P9-DNW-011

Flying
Visits

by the same author

Autobiography
UNRELIABLE MEMOIRS

Fiction
BRILLIANT CREATURES

Verse
PEREGRINE PRYKKE'S PILGRIMAGE
THROUGH THE LONDON LITERARY WORLD

THE FATE OF FELICITY FARK
IN THE LAND OF THE MEDIA

BRITANNIA BRIGHT'S BEWILDERMENT
IN THE WILDERNESS OF WESTMINSTER

CHARLES CHARMING'S CHALLENGES
ON THE PATHWAY TO THE THRONE

FAN-MAIL
POEM OF THE YEAR

Criticism
THE METROPOLITAN CRITIC
VISIONS BEFORE MIDNIGHT
AT THE PILLARS OF HERCULES
THE CRYSTAL BUCKET
FIRST REACTIONS
FROM THE LAND OF SHADOWS
GLUED TO THE BOX

*Collections of lyrics set and sung by
Pete Atkin on the RCA label*
BEWARE OF THE BEAUTIFUL STRANGER
DRIVING THROUGH MYTHICAL AMERICA
A KING AT NIGHTFALL
THE ROAD OF SILK
SECRET DRINKER
THE RIDER TO THE WORLD'S END
LIVE LIBEL
MASTER OF THE REVELS

Flying Visits

Postcards from the Observer 1976–83

Clive James

W·W·NORTON & COMPANY

New York   London

This collection first published 1984
Copyright © 1976, 1977, 1978, 1979, 1980, 1982, 1983, 1984 by the Observer
Introduction copyright © 1984 by Clive James
Printed in the United States of America.

First American Edition, 1986

Library of Congress Cataloging-in-Publication Data

James Clive, 1939-
Flying visits.

1. Voyages and travels—1951-   —Addresses,
essays, lectures. 2. Air travel—Addresses, essays,
lectures. I. Title.
G465.J355   1986   910.4   85-21599

ISBN 0-393-02294-3

W. W. Norton & Company, Inc., 500 Fifth Avenue, New York, N.Y. 10110

W. W. Norton & Company Ltd., 37 Great Russell Street, London WC1B 3NU

1 2 3 4 5 6 7 8 9 0

To Martin Amis

Then, forehead against the pane, I suddenly feel
The longing open-armed behind the bone
To drown myself in other worlds, to steal
All lives, all times, all countries not my own.

Francis Hope, *Schlossbesuch*

Contents

Author's Note

THESE articles, along with some of the Introduction, appeared in the *Observer* from time to time between 1976 and 1983. Here and there I have restored some small cuts which had to be made if the piece was to fit the page, but otherwise I have added very little. The occasional outright howler has been corrected, but only if it was a matter of detail which I should have got right in the first place. Hindsight would have allowed further improvements but there would have been no end to the process. In the second article about China, for example, it seemed likely at the time, and for some time after, that the Hong Kong dollar would hold up. A year later, the Peking mandarins having proved intractable, it fell. If I were to rewrite the piece so as to predict this fact, it would become a claim to prescience, or at any rate no longer a report written at that moment. But like any other flying visitor, in the Far East or anywhere else, I was there at that moment, ignorant as to what would happen next, and fully occupied with making the most elementary sense of what had happened already. That has been the real story of mass jet travel: the world opening up to people who have no qualifications for exploring it except the price of a ticket. But I have never been able to believe that all my fellow tourists were quite blind. Even a postcard can be written with point.

C.J.

London, 1984

Two postcards have been added but nothing altered. Since the British edition went to press, the Hong Kong dollar has gone back up again, thereby restoring my predictions on the subject to a seeming accuracy. But the casual mention, in the same piece, of Mrs Thatcher's breakfast meeting with Mrs Gandhi in Delhi, has subsequently been rendered flippant. With the rest of Mrs Thatcher's press entourage I stood just outside the front gate of the house where Mrs Gandhi was later to be murdered by her guards, but there was no guessing. There rarely is – although if you fear everything, some of it will come true. Grenades went off on Temple Mount in Jerusalem a week after I stood there, but a miss is as good as a mile.

The same applies to disaster in the air. The number of Boeing 747s in the world, cited in the text as almost three hundred, is by now almost six hundred. A few have recently been subtracted from the total. Each time it was like a small town going missing. But my praise of the aircraft's beauty and strength remains valid. The actual airframe was seldom at fault, and the number of accidents, from all causes, for the 747 or any other big civil aircraft, is vanishingly small compared to the huge number of flights completed with no more damage to the passengers than swollen feet and the boredom of seeing *Cannonball Run II* several times in the same month.

If you were to spend as much time in the air as you do at the office, you would still be safer than if you were to spend as much time on the road as you do in the air. It remains true that even the worst driver gives up his chance of influencing events when he commits himself to the care of even the best pilot. To be apprehensive when helpless is only to be human. Francis Hope, the gifted young British poet, critic and political commentator quoted in the epigraph, died in the notorious Turkish Airlines DC-10 crash outside Paris. Those of us in his generation of journalists have had good reason to think of his demise as our passports fill up and have to be replaced. But such a casual disappearance should make one fear fate, not flying, which continues, for me at least, to be a relaxing experience, especially now that I have learned to supplement the in-flight entertainment with my own cassette player. Seven miles up with no telephone ringing is a good place for listening to Debussy.

On my first flights I used to help the aircraft into the air by pulling on the armrests, and help it land by holding the seat steady with my braced thighs. Repetition has soothed the nerves, until now I feel as safe as houses. Not that I feel particularly safe in houses any more, but that might be just a case of getting the world in proportion, a process which air travel can only encourage.

C.J.

London, 1985

Flying
Visits

Introduction

THERE is a bad kind of travel writer who complains that the airport he leaves from herds him like a sheep, that the airliner he travels on feeds and lulls him like a veal calf, and that the airport he arrives at herds him like a sheep all over again, with the additional insult of somehow concealing all the allegedly exotic wonders that would have been revealed to him had he been allowed to make landfall by sampan or on the back of a camel.

To complain that modern travel has become a cliché is a cliché in itself. It is also an especially conceited brand of romanticism, by which you imagine yourself in the curled shoes and flowing robes of Sir Richard Burton or T.E. Lawrence. Such adventures were already beyond recapture when they were first heard about, since new ground can be broken only once. Anyway, in this as in any other field, reality should be romance enough. I like airports and airliners. Nor is this a case of frankly admitting to myself, as with my fond feelings for television, an enthusiasm that was always there but masked by intellectual snobbery. There was never any hope of generating enough intellectual snobbery to cover up my keenness for the airways.

I was already enslaved when the old compound-engined Douglas DC-6Bs were shaking my house to pieces back in the early Fifties. The house, situated in the Sydney suburb of Kogarah, lay among the approach lights to what was then the main runway of Kingsford-Smith airport – or aerodrome, as it was always called in those days. Before attaining long trousers I could already identify, from the engine note alone, the DC-4, every variety of the DC-6, the Lockheed Constellation, the Convair 240 and the Boeing Stratocruiser. They all rattled the crockery but the DC-6B could crack a Pyrex casserole dish. When the first Stratocruiser arrived via Hawaii, to the accompaniment of a tremendous publicity campaign from Pan Am, I had already been camped for two days in the sand dunes about a hundred yards from where it was due to touch down. Other members of my gang were hollow-eyed from hearing me tell them all about the wonder plane's double-bubble pressure hull, but they looked appropriately awe-stricken when the huge machine descended right in front of us, belching gouts of flame from the exhausts of its Twin Wasp radials. Essentially a B-29 bomber nine months pregnant, the Stratocruiser was far from being the world's most elegant airliner, but it seemed to me aesthetically pleasing beyond anything I had ever known, and even today I can hear the pained squeal from the tyres of the main undercarriage as they hit the tarmac and started rolling at 100 m.p.h. plus.

Those old piston-engined airliners would have fascinated me even had they never left the ground, but the thought of such beautiful mechanisms actually travelling through the sky was almost too much to take. In those days, flying was an activity for grown-up, fabulously wealthy people with deep voices: to my knowledge nobody in short pants had ever been allowed the freedom of the air. But one could haunt the airport at weekends, and one did. All through my early teens I was down at the airport on Saturday afternoons making myself indispensable to the cleaners sweeping out the planes. Although I was careful always to wear an old leather flying helmet in order to blend into the ambience, somehow my daydream of being asked to replace a sick co-pilot ('Think you can handle it, son?') never came true, and indeed I was not to get airborne until many years later. But I saw the flight-decks of most of the piston-engined airliners up to and including the Super Constellation, a version of the original Constellation which had been so often 'stretched' that its shadow going over our house perceptibly lowered the air temperature.

Older now, the proud smoker of several cigarettes a day, I was there again in the sand dunes when the first Boeing 707 landed, ushering in the intercontinental jet era that should have begun with the de Havilland Comet but tragically did not. My theoretical allegiance was to the British designers, but emotionally there was only one thing to do about the 707 – gape in wonder. Kingsford-Smith's old main runway was not long enough to take the new plane so the transverse strip was extended out into Botany Bay, thereby preserving our house from the cataclysmic effect of the twice-weekly Pan Am 707 flight from Los Angeles. In fact the 707, though noisier than the later wide-bodies, made nothing like the racket kicked up by the piston engines of all those stretched post-war classics that had been fragmenting my mother's china for the previous decade. Jet roar has no throb in it – it can howl but it doesn't hammer. Nevertheless the good people of Kogarah were glad to be no longer in the blast path. All except me.

Farewelling an early girl-friend on her Pan Am 707 flight back to America, I stood heavy-hearted as the plane took off, not because she was going without me but because she was going instead. The aircraft looked powerful enough to reach the Moon. The wheels came up, the flaps retracted, and you could see the flexible wings take the weight as the plane went spearing up through the heat-wobble. Imagine how it must feel. Alas, imagine was all I could afford. When I left for England the means of transport was a rusty old ship that took five weeks to get there. Then there were two or three years in London when I scarcely earned enough to catch a no. 27 bus. But eventually I found myself getting airborne, not – emphatically not – because I had become rich, but because air travel was expanding to embrace the poor.

The Sixties were the great age of the charter flight. Before the wide-bodies had ever been invented, mass air travel was already under way. You could get to Milan, for example, for a very small amount of money if you were a student. The

3

planes were ageing Britannias and even older Douglas DC-7Cs belonging to unknown airlines operating from tin sheds at the wind-swept edges of Gatwick or Luton, and most of your fellow students turned out to be ninety-year-old Calabrian peasant women in black clothes carrying plucked chickens. On my first flight I was petrified when we took off, largely because I had made the mistake of looking out of the window at the moment when the pilot arrived by Jeep. He was wearing an eye-patch, walked with a stiff leg and saluted the aircraft with what appeared to be an aluminium hand. Around his neck the silver brassard of a Polish award for bravery gleamed in the weak sunlight. But in the air I was too busy to be afraid. The ancient dwarf nun in the seat beside me – one of my fellow students – had never flown before in her life except when dreaming of the Last Judgment. Her rosary clattered in her gnarled hands like a football fan's rattle and when the plane tilted to avoid the Matterhorn she sang a brief excerpt from a Donizetti aria before being sick into her plastic carrier-bag full of new potatoes. I got the job of holding her hand while the heavily loaded plane crabbed sideways on the wind and hit the runway between the two long lines of gutted old DC-4s which in those days told you that you were landing at Malpensa, Milan's second best airport. At Linate, the first best, we would probably not have been allowed to land even if on fire.

Other early flights were equally hair-raising but somehow I never seemed to mind. There was a way of flying to Paris which involved a long bus-ride from London to a grass-strip airfield terminating at the Kentish cliffs, an even longer bus-ride from the French coast to Paris, and, between the two bus rides, an incredibly short hop across the Channel. The airborne sector of the trip was accomplished in a high-wing twin-engined British airliner whose make I will not specify, lest you take fright and cancel if you ever find yourself booked on one of the few surviving examples. No doubt it is a perfectly good aircraft in normal circumstances, but with a full load including me it took so long to get off the ground on the British side that one felt one might as well have stayed on the bus. Once again I made the mistake of looking out of the window, this time as the aircraft was pitching and yawing over the bumpy grass and dodging at full power between blasé sheep towards the cliff edge. A rabbit popped out of its hole, looked at me, and overtook us.

It was worth it just to be airborne, even if that particular flight rose only just far enough over the English Channel to clear the upper works of Greek oil tankers steaming towards each other. I used to spend all those early flights with my nose squashed against the window. Nowadays I have learned the trick of always asking for an aisle seat, so that if you have a drunken Bulgarian hammer-thrower sitting beside you at least you won't have to climb over him to get to the toilet. But in those days I wanted to see everything happening outside, even when what was happening outside was too close to the inside for comfort. You never knew when there would be a revelation. At night the cities were like jewelled cobwebs on black velvet. Coming back from Venice on a BEA Comet 4 night flight, as one of the only two passengers aboard, I was invited to the flight deck just at the right moment to see the lights of Paris. Stacking around Gatwick in a chartered Britannia while the pilot negotiated through an interpreter for permission to land, I saw an old Elizabethan – one of the loveliest aeroplanes ever made – slip out of the cloud 1,000 feet below us. I presume our aircraft waggled its wings out of recognition rather than surprise. There was always something to look at, even if it was only a sea of cloud, and the more often you flew the more were the chances of an epiphany, such as the occasional clear day over the Alps when there was nothing under you except naked geology up which girls in dirndls ran yodelling, while the jet engines worked their continuous invisible miracle of plaiting cold air into a rope of power.

As for the airports, even the low-rent, secondary ones turned out to be more congenial than the propaganda would have had you believe. After I learned the trick of carrying

5

nothing much except hand baggage and nothing much in
that except a few good books, I quite enjoyed the delays.
Even within the confines of Europe, the idea that all airports
were the same turned out to be exactly wrong. In fact any
airport anywhere immediately reflects the political system,
economic status and cultural characteristics of the country
where it is situated. During the supposedly swinging Sixties,
both of the major London airports gave you a dauntingly
accurate picture of Britain's true condition, with one delay
leading to another, a permanent total breakdown of the
information service supposedly responsible for telling you all
about it, and food you would not have given to a dog. Zurich
airport, on the other hand, was like a bank which had merged
with a hospital in order to manufacture chocolates. At Milan
and Rome, the radar operators went on strike during a fog,
and the security police, all armed with automatic weapons,
stood posing dramatically while Arab terrorists walked past
them carrying dismantled bazookas in golf bags. Salzburg
airport was full of pictures of Herbert von Karajan, thus
providing a useful introduction to a city which depends on
him economically, derives its cultural justification from his
mere existence, and bakes cakes the shape of his head. And at
Moscow's Sheremetsevo, the sheer number of Aeroflot jet
airliners parked in lines told you something about the size of
the country, the conspicuous lack of things to buy in the
airport shops told you a lot about its economy, and the sullen
vindictiveness with which the female customs inspectors
went through the luggage of their compatriots returning from
abroad told you all you needed to know about how fairly the
shares had been dealt out. I watched a blue-uniformed lady
looking like Geoff Capes in a wig taking a young man's newly
acquired pig-skin luggage apart, laying out his rich assort-
ment of silk ties and stroking one by one a plump heap of
cashmere scarves. Both of them settled down for a long,
painful interview. You could see why Russian diplomats, on
their first trip outside the Soviet Union, sometimes break
down and cry in Copenhagen airport, unable to cope with

the mere sight of the consumer goods on the glass shelves.

I finally got a trip on a Boeing 707 at just the time it was about to go out of style, because the first wide-bodies were already proving their routes. But it was still a thrill, not least because the destination was Boston – a long way from Europe. Over mid-Atlantic a BOAC VC-10 going the other way went past a few miles to our left on my side of the aircraft, and a mile or so above. The condensation trail came out of the cobalt blue distance like a spear of snow. As we let down into Boston, I watched the magic suitcase of the Boeing wing unpack itself, the flaps jacking out and curving down to turn the aerofoil into a parasol. It was a long time since I had bought *Flight* magazine every week and memorised the contents, but I was still clued-up enough to be aware that the same wing had held the B-52s up in the sky while they split the ground of South-East Asia and drove a lot of little children crazy just with the noise. There is good reason for thinking we are alive in a particularly shameful stretch of history, the only era in which the innocent have ever been obliterated on an industrial basis. But on the airliners and in the airports I found myself unable to pretend that I did not enjoy living in the twentieth century. You will find an extermination camp in the seventh book of Thucydides. People have always destroyed each other on as grand a scale as the prevailing technology allowed. But powered flight has all happened within a single lifetime. Recently I had dinner with a man who remembered crossing the Atlantic on the old *Aquitania* in 1903, the year the Wright brothers first flew at Kittyhawk. Even Leonardo, who could do anything, could only dream of flying. And here was I, without even a licence to drive a car, riding down out of the sky into Massachusetts after having crossed the Atlantic in a few hours. A king of infinite space, I was justifiably annoyed when the immigration officer sent me back to fill out my form again because I had not pressed hard enough to ink the carbon copy.

Then the wide-bodies came in and the age of mass aerial migration was on for young and old. By those who flew them the wide-bodies were known as heavies and the name was soon in use among such non-practising pilots as myself. The DC-10 I found hard to love at first, especially after one of them crashed near Paris and killed a lot of people, including someone I knew. The Tristar I found disconcertingly hard to tell apart from the DC-10, until I learned to remember that the DC-10 was the one with the third engine half-way up its tail. Twenty years earlier I would have learned a hundred different recognition points but as you get older other things usurp your attention. There was no difficulty, however, about spotting which of the three principal heavies was the winner. Nobody with a proper appreciation of the Boeing 747's looks will ever call it a Jumbo. The 747 is so suavely proportioned that it doesn't even look very big, except when it happens to taxi past its ancestor, the 707, whereupon you feel that a mackerel has given birth to a mako shark.

Loved by pilots for its handling qualities and seemingly infinite reserves of getaway, the 747 flies like a fighter and at first glance even looks like one. In fact it looks a lot like the old F-86 Sabre, with its flight-deck bulge perched right forward like a Sabre's bubble canopy and the same proud angle to its tail feathers. On the ground the 747 is perhaps a bit fussy underneath, like a house being moved around on a lot of roller skates, but when it gets into the air, cleans itself up, and pours on the 100,000 horsepower of its turbofans, there is nothing less awkward or lovelier aloft. Unless you had been told, you would never think of it as having 400 people on board. It looks as if there is only one man in there, having the time of his life.

Like millions of other travellers I soon got used to walking on board a heavy and going anywhere I felt like in a straight line. But when the straight line was stretched around a curved world it sometimes meant that if the eventual destination was Tokyo or Los Angeles then you had to spend a couple of hours at Anchorage, Alaska. Sharing with Bahrain the distinction of being an airport from which absolutely no transit passenger ever gets the urge to take a taxi into town, Anchorage is like a British Rail waiting-room equipped with kiosks flogging Eskimo artefacts made in Taiwan and large segments of duty-free raw fish which the Japanese buy gift-wrapped. You will see half a dozen Japanese team up to buy the component pieces of a killer whale. From a glass case a stuffed polar bear looks on, beady-eyed with boredom. But if you bag a plastic seat near the window and look up into the sky, you will see the heavies queueing to land. When the air is clear you can see them stacked up, a couple of minutes behind one another, all the way to the stratosphere.

The greatest number of heavies I ever saw in one place was at New York's Kennedy airport after a storm. There are almost 400 747s in the world and it looked as if half of them were queueing to get away. Unfortunately I was in one of them and so didn't get a very good look. The best airports to watch big jets taking off at are those in which a single main building parallels a solitary runway. Dubai gives you an excellent show, especially at night. While the locals snatch a quick kip on the floor of the coffee lounge, you can take a window seat and enjoy an uninterrupted view of a heavy full of furiously praying pilgrims rolling out of nowhere and heading straight up.

Dubai is a very good-looking airport, whose Moorish formality, like a bleached Alhambra minus the filigrees, suggests the controlling hand of an Arab designer conscious of his heritage. In fact the architectural firm involved was English. On the other hand, Saudi Arabia's Dharan airport, which looks just like Dubai, was dreamed up by Minoni Yamasaki, the same Japanese architect who designed New York's Trade Center. Aesthetic considerations have become more important now that the hazards which once gave airports their individuality have perforce been eliminated. There are not many airports left like Hong Kong's Kai Tak, and even there the precise ground control has made the wing-and-a-prayer element illusory, although the illusion can be hair-raising on a stormy evening when the pilot seems intent on flying you into a hillside tunnel. In the old piston-engined days, if Chicago's O'Hare airport had cloud down to the deck the pilots on their approach leg used to correct for drift by the neon sign on Joe's Diner. No such news comes out of Chicago today. When there is a big tangle on the ground, it usually, as at Tenerife, happens under a clear sky, with all the right signals being given but one man out of his senses. At Madrid it happened in a fog but that was an exception – even at Madrid.

While you sit in the airport coffee-lounge killing time, it is extremely unlikely that the aeroplanes you watch will be killing people. One pilot might have a heart-attack while climbing away, another might complete his landing run in an adjacent suburb – both those things have happened near London in my time – but usually at the airport itself you will be offered only the subtler forms of drama. They can be very pleasing. At Tullamarine airport in Melbourne you can sit high up in the terminal building and see the whole take-off run with nothing in the background except unspoiled country. The experience is easier on the eyes than anything they are likely to encounter in the cabin once you get air-borne, unless you are flying with Singapore Airlines, whose stewardesses really are as advertised. They are far more beautiful than they need to be and in First Class there seem to be two of them assigned to each passenger, filling him continuously with delicious food and bursting discreetly into tears if he stops eating. The Singapore commitment to the putative beauty of air travel verges on the mystical, and not just in the air. The same applies to Changi airport, which is currently the second most beautiful piece of aerospace architecture in the world. But after admiring the indoor fountains and having been suitably dazed by the shops full of microchip prosperity, you might need something to read. Relax: your needs are catered for. The bookstalls all carry several different biographies of Lee Kwan Yew, whom Singapore has got the way Salzburg has got Karajan. But somehow, read in that glittering context, Lee's story becomes exciting instead of tedious, in the same way that the coffee tastes better than it should. It is because there are so many aircraft in the vicinity. Airfields made even Kafka happy: his *Die Aeroplane in Brescia* of 1909 is a cry of love. Proust was mad about airports until his beloved Agostinelli wrote himself off in a crash.

The most beautiful piece of aerospace architecture on earth – no ifs, buts or cults of personality – is undoubtedly Narita, which has now replaced Haneda as Tokyo's number one airport. The students did all they could to stop Narita being built, but now that the *fait* is *accompli* it is hard not to be glad. Haneda was a health hazard and Narita is a work of art. The main building is one vast, deceptively simple arrangement of glass and distance, while the runways at night are a ravishing display of emeralds, sapphires and rubies. Heading south from Narita in a JAL DC-10, I climbed unharmed through miles of sky which had once been full of screaming danger. Here was where the last great strategic battles between aircraft that the world will ever see were fought out to the bitter end. The Japanese, improvising desperately against time, built fighters that could fly just high and fast enough to knock B-29-*san* down. But as Admiral Yamamoto had realised before Pearl Harbor, the war was lost before it started. High over Saipan, whose defenders once fought all the more savagely for having no chances left, I knew just enough Japanese to ask the hostess for more coffee (*Kohi aramas ka?*) and she knew just enough English to ask me if I wanted a hot towel (You rike hot taoaroo?). As cultural contact goes it might not have amounted to a securely united world but it beat having to drop bombs on her.

The airliners haven't shrunk the earth. Going all the way around it still feels like a journey. But they have turned it into one place. Beyond the airport boundaries, each country remains odd enough to satisfy anybody's thirst for strangeness. Meanwhile the airports hint at a world which might become peaceful simply by being too pointlessly busy to do anything else. My only regret is that I will probably be too old for space. I have done my best to snare a window seat on an early space shuttle but so far they are being niggardly with the tickets. To go up so far that there is no down is still one of my dreams of heaven.

Meanwhile, as always, there is poetry enough in the here and now. All I do for a living is put words beside each other but I have been shown wonders without even asking. With raw egg dropping from chopsticks into my lap I have looked down on the North Pole. Over the Persian Gulf at midnight I have looked down and seen the oil rigs burning like the damned. Best of all, I have found that every way you fly leads home. Crossing the paralysed red rock ocean of Australia's Dead Heart as the sun comes up, Qantas flight QF2 lets down over Sydney Harbour before the morning glare has burned the pale-blue summer mist off the silver water. Over there on the right is my house, the sideboard now full of intact crockery.

Nowadays I go home too often to get particularly excited about it, but I was fifteen years in Europe before I first made the trip back, with the result that the two pieces about Sydney at the start of this book are perhaps slightly over-wrought. My home country struck me not so much with its foreignness as with a familiarity I had not taken sufficient notice of in the first place: hence the uneasy urge to pontificate. But Donald Trelford, newly appointed as the *Observer's* Editor, graciously announced that I had stumbled on a new format: the Postcard, which might be written not just from Australia but from anywhere in the world I could get to in those few weeks of the year when I wasn't sitting in the London dark reviewing television. In the age of jet-lag most travel pieces by a non-resident correspondent were condemned to impressionism anyway. The last thing a visiting fireman could do was to investigate the causes of the fire. Leave that to the man on the spot. The Postcard writer would make a virtue of necessity. Wherever he was, he would be there for only a few days, but nowadays the same applied to almost everyone. Now that first impressions were common currency, they counted more than ever. Get them down and bring them home.

Which is pretty well what I did. The Postcards are arranged chronologically and the reader will discover, if he keeps going, that the writer became less and less inclined to wax sententious, asked fewer and fewer important people for their considered views, and grew more and more shameless about doing corny tourist things, down to and including the guided tour of the catacombs and the pool-side barbecue billed to your room. Somewhere out there in the allegedly shrinking world I lost some of my pride.

It could have been because my curiosity was expanding. Life is so various that the first things you notice will be strange enough to go on with. At any foreign airport you will meet your sophisticated compatriot who will tell you that everything you are about to see is a cliché and that the real life is behind the scenes. But he himself is the cliché. You will learn more from the local man with the bad shave who sells dark glasses. One hot afternoon on the West Bank near Alara, a Palestinian taxi-driver showed me his house. It was Ramadan, so the children could look at the cakes his wife was preparing but were not allowed to eat them. I, on the other hand, was not allowed *not* to eat them. In the glass-fronted tall oak-veneer cabinet against the living-room wall, sets of coloured glass tumblers and cups were displayed in their original cardboard cartons. He was making something of his life but either didn't believe that he would be doing worse under Arab rule or else thought it irrelevant. Eventually, he hoped, the Arab nations would destroy Israel, but meanwhile the British would combine with the Americans and turn against his people, unless Lord Carrington came back as Foreign Secretary. I couldn't think of a polite way to tell him of my suspicion that the Middle East problem was no longer high on Lord Carrington's roster of priorities. Helping to keep me tongue-tied was the inescapable fact that this man was myself under another name. He had merely been born somewhere else, and in less kind circumstances. The main difference between us was that I had seen something of the world. The main hope for the future is that his children will see something of it too. That chaos in the airports is our chance to live.

Postcard from Sydney

1 Home, James

CHUGGING through the stratosphere for twenty-four hours from London to Sydney, the Qantas Boeing 747 *City of Newcastle* did its best to keep us all happy, but apart from watching *The French Connection Part II* and consuming the numberless meals delivered to one's lap by the hardest-working cabin staff in the history of aviation, there was little to do except make increasingly feeble attempts to keep one's children out of mischief and go to the toilet.

This every single one of the several hundred passengers did at least a dozen times on the voyage, making a total of many thousands of separate visits. Queues for the loo stretched down every aisle. It was somewhere between Bombay and Perth that the vision hit me. Our enormous aircraft, the apotheosis of modern technology, was filling up with gunk! Converted into chemical inertia by the cobalt-blue reagent in the flushing water, the waste products of our skyborne community were gradually taking over the plane!

I adduce the above fantasy only to demonstrate the intensity with which one hallucinates after nearly a full day in the sky on the long haul out to one's homeland. I had been fifteen years away from Australia. While I had been gone, the whole of the modern phase of Australian politics had taken place. The Gough Whitlam revolution – often called a 'renaissance', to emphasise its air of cultural euphoria – had been and gone. The same conservative forces were now back in power as had ruled the country so suffocatingly when I left. How much had I missed out on? And what if, despite my unfortunate timing, the place had indeed altered past recognition? Trepidations about culture-shock were eased only by the knowledge that the captain of our aircraft was called

Barry Tingwell. The sheer Australianness of that name was as antipodean as a sand-fly bite or a sting from a jelly-blubber.

In fact culture-shock had already begun a few nights before I left London, when I had seen the National Theatre's *Hamlet* and Barry Humphries' opening night as Edna Everage in the same thrill-packed evening. From the *Hamlet*, an austerity production in British Army standard-issue boots, to Edna's non-stop spectacular, with its voluptuous wealth of sequins and gladioli, had already been a large step from the old rigour to the new expansiveness. As Hamlet, Albert Finney had lacked lustre. As Edna, Barry Humphries had had lustre to burn. Edna's Proustian savouring of the *things* in her rich life – the gaudy catalogue of Australiana she carries in her dizzy head – was a call from the homeland as imperative as Penelope's sigh. Thus it was that Barry Tingwell steered me south-east around the curve of the world.

The first view of Australia was the coast near Perth: reefs, white beaches, shallow water like the juice of emeralds. In the suburbs, hundreds of swimming pools the colour of Paul Newman's eyes attested to affluence. But then, I had never seen Perth before. Perhaps it had always been like that. The transcontinental haul was fascinating to one who had never flown over Australia before in his life. (I had come to Europe by ship: a five-week voyage costing about £60 sterling. In those days everybody you knew was too poor to fly.) Look at those circular salt lakes, each a separate colour like the little tubs of paint in a child's paint-box! But an Australian businessman in a short-sleeved suit who had got on with a blast of reminiscent heat at Perth explained that this was nothing – the really fantastic scenery was further north. I should try it some time. Perhaps I should, and one day shall: but I felt resistant. For this trip, the eastern seaboard would be enough, and I wasn't even sure I could manage that. For the first time I was becoming physically aware of how far-flung the land was into which I had been born. There had been another change of pilots at Perth. Where was Barry Tingwell? Help.

At Sydney the 747 made its landing approach low over the suburb where I was born and grew up – Kogarah, on Botany Bay. It was night. Sydney was a vast field of lights: since the Aussie's ideal is to own his Own Home, the cities sprawl inordinately. Not all that much less than London, Sydney filled the sky with costume jewellery as the 747 heeled over, shaken by a great inner surge of cerulean goo. The flaps jacked out. The turbofans lapsed from a whine to a grumble. Like a winged supertanker full of odoriferous amethystine ordure the colossal machine brought me back to my roots.

Next morning the roots were on display in bright sunshine. Whatever overtones of unease eventually accrued to my four-week stay in Australia – and I should say in advance that I ended the trip feeling even more of an interloper than when I began – nothing should be allowed to detract from a proper celebration of that first, and continuing, impression of Sydney and its harbour. It remains one of the Earth's truly beautiful places. Apart from the startling Manhattanisation of its business district, the city was more or less as I remembered it, except that for the twenty-one years I lived there I never really appreciated it – one of the big things that can be said in favour of going back, partly offsetting the even bigger things that can be said for remaining an expatriate once you have become one.

The late Kenneth Slessor, in his prose as much as in his poetry, probably came nearest to evoking the sheer pulchritude of Sydney harbour. But finally the place is too multifarious to be captured by the pen. Sydney is like Venice without the architecture, but with more of the sea: the merchant ships sail right into town. In Venice you never see big ships – they are all over at Mestre, the industrial sector. In Sydney big ships loom at the ends of city streets. They are parked all over the place, tied up to the countless wharves in the scores of inlets ('You could hide a thousand ships of the line in here,' a British admiral observed long ago) or just moored to a buoy in mid-harbour, riding high. At the International Terminal at Circular Quay, the liners in which my generation of the self-exiled left for Europe still tie up: from the Harbour Bridge you can look down at the farewell parties raging on their decks. Most important, the ferries are still on the harbour. Nothing like as frequent as they once were, but still there – the perfect way of getting to and from work.

Some of the big Manly ferries have been replaced by hydrofoils, but there are a few of the old ones left. Always the biggest ferries on the harbour, they were built strongly to sail unperturbed through the pelagic swell as they crossed Sydney Heads to Manly. Poems in blond wood and brass fittings, they were named after surfing beaches: Dee Why, South Steyne, Curl Curl. Now there is a fund being raised to save the *South Steyne* from the breakers' yard, while the hulks of some of the others are to be seen lying derelict against the Pyrmont wharves.

Riding across to Manly in the Forties, we used to lean perilously over the balustrade of the open engine-room and watch the reciprocating whatchumacallits clonk and gwerp – 'we' being children in English-style school uniforms of flannel short-trousered suits and long socks. The smell of the machine-oil and the sensual heave of the ferry in the Pacific waves is an abiding memory, which I found unimpaired by repeating the experience as an adult. Towards sunset, when the light strikes the harbour at a shallow angle and turns the water silver, the ferries, their setting deprived of all perspective, hang in space, like long-lensed photographs of themselves: dream-boats.

But where the ferry somehow survived, the tram did not. Melbourne keeps its trams but Sydney had got rid of them long before I left Australia. The toast-rack tram – open to the sun and breeze, full of character and incident – was the best form of street-transport ever invented. Unfortunately it sorted ill with the motor car, which since the early Fifties has ruled the city father's dreams, as if Sydney might be a new Los Angeles horizontally, just as it aspires to be a new New York vertically. It was in this spirit that the Cahill Expressway – a flyover of heroic ugliness named after the same politician who gave birth to the Opera House – was built over Circular Quay, almost totally destroying the atmosphere of what had, after all, once been Sydney Cove, the site of the First Settlement.

Almost, but not quite. More by luck than judgment, Circular Quay kept some of its character, and while I have been away has even increased in interest, due to the effects of an unequivocally positive addition to Sydney's life – immigration. The cosmopolitan, or ethnic, influence on Sydney first of all becomes visible when you notice the amount and kind of fast foods on offer. At the Circular Quay milk bars, where once the most you could hope for in the way of take-away food was a lethal meat pie and a cream bun, you can now take your pick from kateifi, baklava, syrup rolls, honey and almond triangles, Turkish delight and fruit slices. One of the indisputably beneficial European influences – food – has been added to one of the most enduring Australian traditions – the milk-shake. And, as long as you are content to drink your milk-shake on or near the premises, it is still possible to have it prepared as it should be, in a dented silver container battered around the rim from being clipped a million times into the mixing machine.

The completed milk-shake should never be tipped into a glass, but consumed direct from the container, either through a paper straw (with a resonant slurp to mop up the frothy dregs) or by applying the loose mouth to the cold metal and tilting until the blob of ice-cream collides with the top lip. The conflict involved in choosing between these two methods almost always necessitates the purchase of a second milk-shake. While drinking it and eating your pastries, you can lean over the railings between the wharves and watch the sprats feeding underwater around the pilings. At such moments, Sydney offers a *petite bonheur* comparable to anything obtainable in, say, Paris, where there is seldom anywhere comfortable to eat your crêpes, no matter how delicious the chocolate sauce. Stay on, or near, the water and

Sydney's version of the Little Happiness can be very near to Heaven.

When Australians talk about Culture they seldom mean honey and almond triangles. Perhaps they ought to, though. It's in the ordinary facts of everyday life that culture is to be measured – which is why Edna Everage reigns supreme as Australia's greatest cultural commentator, the Raymond Williams of the South Pacific. Australians talk in the one breath about the giant strides made in wine and poetry, but the awkward truth is that while the advance made in Australian wine is beyond dispute, to claim an advance in Australian poetry is largely meaningless. In the minutiae of existence Australia has changed in all sorts of ways since I left home. But in the large abstractions it seems to me to have stayed roughly as it was.

Turn back from leaning over the rails at the Quay and you are looking at Sydney's answer to Manhattan. The tallest building in Sydney when I left is now one of the shortest in the skyline. Photographs of this upsurge had disturbed me in exile but brought up against it I was less impressed. Some of the straining shapes on view are at least original, but even those are usually hideous, and on the whole I'm afraid the vaunted progress of Sydney's business architecture ('Ar, Sydney's coming on,' my old friends have been telling me for years: 'Ya wooden wreckingnise it') bears out the Italian proverb about fifty skyscrapers screwing a city. To the extent that the tall buildings have created space around their podiums they represent what Raymond Williams (the Edna Everage of the North Atlantic) would call a Clear Gain. But on the whole, the city's human scale has been destroyed for the sake of physically reflecting an exultation which was always more like arrogance than self-confidence and which was already fading before Whitlam toppled. Large areas of office-space in the new towers are still for rent and will for a long time stay as empty as Centrepoint in London or the Trade Center in New York.

Such conspicuous waste represents the self-destructive

element in the burgeoning national consciousness. There is a creative element too, but it works within a more modest range. The care with which the Rocks area of Sydney has been preserved is a good example of the creative element in action.

By now the awareness that there are things to be cherished is widespread, like a taste for wine, which is no longer restricted to the travelled minority. (Nor, of course, is travel.) The wine buff can order his tipple at 30 dollars a dozen before the grapes are picked, with right of refusal at the first tasting: it's like putting your son down for Eton. But even the uninstructed are not likely to pass the stuff up when flagon wine at least as good as what goes into the carafes in a restaurant in Italy works out at 20 cents a bottle. In other words, it's free.

It's in these things – in food and drink and places to be and ways to behave – that Australia has come on since my time. But in more grandiose matters – matters where national consciousness is really self-consciousness – the results are more equivocal. Culture with a small c is doing all right. Culture with a capital C has lost its erstwhile diffidence, but in many instances seems to have replaced it with a bombast equally parochial. The Sydney Opera House is a case in point. *The* case in point, because in daring to suggest that there is something wrong with the Opera House, you run the risk of appearing to deny the whole country its right to an identity – a slur not easily forgiven.

Back in England and safe from physical reprisal, it now seems possible to say aloud what I scarcely dared breathe in Australia, even to my relations: that the Opera House is a dud. In the matter of its appearance I have no very strong opinion. To me it looks like a portable typewriter full of oyster shells, and to the contention that it echoes the sails of yachts on the harbour I can only point out that the yachts on the harbour don't waste any time echoing opera houses. But really it is quibbling to talk about the way the thing looks. What matters is the way it works. And for its nominal purpose it doesn't work, and never can.

During the time that I was in Sydney there were no operas scheduled, but I did see a ballet – *The Sleeping Beauty* – sufficiently big to test the opera auditorium's facilities. (There are two auditoria: the smaller one for opera, and the larger one for concerts, including concert versions of those operas too large to fit into the smaller one.) They failed the test. It was embarrassing to see the *corps de ballet* queueing up to get off, there being very little wing-space for them to disappear into. The flimsiness of the décor and the tension in the dancing could all be traced to simple lack of room.

The effort which was poured into finishing the edifice after its architect was fired should not be discounted, even though the American Beauty upholstery in the concert hall (in the opera hall it's tomato red) might not be to one's taste. But similarly it is foolish to suppose that all would have been well had Utzon remained in charge.

The farce began at the beginning, in that first flush of enthusiasm at Utzon's preliminary designs. The judges fell in love with an idea without grasping its substance, thereby acting out in little – or, financially speaking, in large – the Australian attitude to Culture. That attitude is likely to go on generating unintentional humour in large amounts. But since to some extent I once shared that attitude myself, I'm not entirely whole-hearted about joining in the laughter.

June 20, 1976

Footnote By now I feel much more affectionate about the Opera House but the first impression recorded above is probably the more objective. If a Wagner orchestra has to be reduced in size to fit the pit, what you have got is an edifice which does less than the one at Bayreuth at a thousand times the cost. But it looks better: there is no denying that.

Postcard from Sydney

2 Here Is the Noos

'ROASTED in coconut oil and lightly salted, you'll enjoy the smooth richness, the unique flavour of this entirely Australian nut.' This masculine rubric, with its hefty pair of dangling participles, appears on the 500 gram tins of Macadamia nuts now on sale in my homeland. Firm, fleshy and sensual, the Macadamia nut (accent on the third syllable – Maca*day*mia) is the perfect nut. The first person to import Macadamia nuts into Britain will make a million pounds. Once you start eating them there is no way of stopping until you faint.

When I left Australia fourteen years ago, the only way of getting at the kernel of the Macadamia was with a large hammer, since the nut came equipped with a casing of the same dimensions and consistency as ball-bearing ammunition. If you swung the hammer absolutely vertically the casing fractured and the kernel rolled away. If your swing was even slightly angled, the nut disappeared with the sound of a ricocheting bullet, and you might see an old lady collapse in the street, clutching her forehead. While I have been away, someone has found a commercially practicable method of stripping the casings from the kernels. Presumably the casings are then sold as railway ballast or shrapnel. The delicious kernels go into tins, which the people may purchase, thereby enriching their lives. The sum of such small leaps forward – and there have been many – represents Cultural Advance.

Whether there has been Cultural Advance in the grander sense is another question. During the Whitlam era it was taken as axiomatic that Australia was expanding on all fronts, realising its creative potential in every direction after decades of stifling conservatism. Both economically and artistically it was supposed to be boom time. And even now – especially now – that the economic on-rush has faltered, the cultural explosion is taken to be an irreversible gain. The concept of cultural advance is clung to desperately by an intelligentsia still trying to cope with the glaring fact that the same people who voted Whitlam in voted him out again when they began to fear that his liberalising policies would involve them in becoming less rich.

The intelligentsia has been so traumatised by Whitlam's fall that it has placed the blame everywhere except on the people's democratic right to be self-interested. It has tried to blame the Murdoch Press (which is indeed, in its home country, a wonderfully petty organisation), Sir John Kerr, Malcolm Fraser and – in wilder moments – the CIA. But no amount of fulminating can alter the fact that Australia's economy is in a slump for which the people are just as likely to blame Whitlam as to blame Fraser. The intellectuals have perforce gone back to their erstwhile condition of feeling ranged against, rather than with, Government. Like the JFK intellectuals after their hero's assassination, they have lost their power to influence politics directly and now must cultivate their own garden. It is no surprise that they cultivate it with hurt pride, small humour and a greater determination than ever to pronounce Australia independent of all debts to Europe.

But to a great degree, independence from Europe seems to have involved dependence on America, in the small change of culture if not in the large. And since the small change of culture indubitably affects everybody's life, whereas larger cultural matters are for the few and often putative even for them, it is Americanism that nowadays strikes you first about the quotidian tone of Australian existence. A signboard on a unisex hairdresser's shop apostrophises: 'Guys! Gals!' The Sydney traffic signs, which used to be just red, green and amber lights, now say 'WALK/DON'T WALK'. A church advertises 'the friendliest modern worship experience'. When I queried something at the reception desk of a Melbourne hotel the girl on duty said she'd 'check it out'.

Such Americanisation of the language is much more significantly pervasive than the high incidence of skate-boards and roadside fast food parlours. The Australian eastern seaboard is one long Fun City for surfers and wherever there is surf in the world there must inevitably be skate-boards. And the car-trips between towns are very long, so California-style roadside refreshment makes sense, even if the chiko roll – one of the staple fast foods to have emerged since my time – looks and tastes like something which has been slowly passed through a live dog. McDonald's and Kentucky Fried Chicken are everywhere in Australia, but then they're everywhere in Britain too, all set to drive the Wimpy into the sea. The American invasion of the Australian stomach was always on the cards. But the invasion of the language is less easy to laugh off.

The incursion is most noticeable on television. Australian TV is so bad it is almost impossible to describe. If you have seen American television and can imagine it without its redeeming features, then Australian TV is even worse than that. On Australian TV, 'It's A Knock-Out' (retitled 'Almost Anything Goes' and deprived of even the element of literacy conferred on the British version by Stuart Hall and Eddie Waring) rates as highbrow. The locally conceived product is qualitatively shown up by a few imported British series and quantitatively overwhelmed by Americana. 'Homicide', acted with scarcely believable stiffness in front of cardboard sets and taped in black and white, is a representative home-grown series: it makes 'The Streets of San Francisco' look urgent. With the run-of-the-mill stuff so bad, there is no chance for the occasional prestige venture to be any good, since nobody – especially not the actors – is in practice.

Apart from such fitful indigenous efforts, everything and

everybody on television is American-derived, including most
of the link-men. I remember when Australian TV got started
in the Fifties, all the radio newscasters who wanted to get into
it raced off to Hawaii and came back a week later with names
like Chuck Faulkner and accents to match. 'Here is the noos.'
All that still goes on, only more so. During my visit the big
TV event was the filming (and, after a two-week editing
session in California, the screening) of an episode of 'Mc-
Cloud' set in Sydney. Less substantial even than usual –
the presence of Australian actors ensuring an extra level
of awkwardness – the episode used Sydney locations. The
heavies threw someone to the sharks and McCloud threw
one of the heavies off the hotel at King's Cross. Inevitably the final shoot-out was at the Opera House. From the
accompanying hoo-ha of publicity it was hard to escape the
impression that Sydney was at last rating as a world-class
metropolis, now that McCloud had been there.

English writers of my acquaintance who were at the Adel-
aide Festival at the same time as I was in Sydney have since
told me that they were continually struck by the way the
Australian assertion of independence was undermined by an
anxiety about being recognised by the rest of the world. It's
an ambivalent, confused attitude: to proclaim Sydney a great
city but never quite believe it yourself until McCloud agrees
with you. The conflict is partly resolved by appealing to
internationalism.

'International' is a vogue word in Australia, like 'situation'
in Britain. Some Australian cabaret artistes still bill themselves as 'London-based', but it is more common for them to
describe themselves as 'international'. Billboards show
Dennis Lillee fiercely endorsing dozens of different products,
his John Newcombe moustache unashamedly Aussie. But on
the billboard next door the Benson & Hedges advertisement
will feature George Lazenby, 'a well-known Australian international'. A newspaper ad will inform you that people with
'international tastes' buy their shirts in Parramatta Road,
Annandale. The anxiety is all-pervasive – even where it is

unnecessary, since in things like men's clothes Australia has more than caught up with the rest of the world. At the time I left Sydney an ordinary Marks and Sparks pullover would still be displayed individually on a chromium stand in the window of a George Street shop. Today it would take Alan Whicker about an hour to duplicate his entire wardrobe of snazzy schmutter, right down to the Gucci accessories – all without leaving the Wentworth Hotel. And in the simple matter of drinking hours Sydney has transformed itself, so that it is now as rare to see a drunk on the streets as it once was common.

But in other matters there is not just plenty of room for anxiety, there is plenty of reason. The Ocker cult is a natural consequence of the attempt to achieve an Australian identity by sheer force of assertion. The Ocker is Barry McKenzie without his creator's controlling irony – a monster who has broken out of Frankenstein's laboratory and run wild. The idea, apparently, is to identify dinkum forthrightness with beer-swilling, prawn-chundering aggression. Barry McKenzie was intended to convey the disturbed naïvety behind the Australian male's parade of male chauvinism, but by the time he has been transformed into the Ocker the intended self-revelations have been forgotten, although the unintended ones are more self-revealing than ever.

For a mercy, Ockerism is derided by the educated young, who buy the post-Woodstock package in its entirety and are by now immune to the cruder forms of populism: their own conformity is more benign. The Ocker is strictly a mass media event – but then Australia is pre-eminently a mass society. Ockerism's most famous incarnation is Paul Hogan, a stand-up comic who rivals even Dennis Lillee as an advertiser's idea of irresistible consumer-bait.

I went to the St George Leagues Club to catch Hogan's act. The Leagues Club, which has doubled in size since my time, more than lived up to its reputation as the biggest thing of its kind in the Southern Hemisphere – although it is difficult to think of any other place in the Southern Hemisphere which might conceivably want to emulate it. Built as a reinforced concrete hymn to the St George Rugby League team (they won the championship for eleven years straight from 1956–66 and there was a time when I could recite the names of the whole side, including the reserves), the place has 40,000 members and looks like an aquarium full of slot machines. Kitsch portraits of front-row forwards with necks wider than their heads are spot-lit in the stairwells. Yet as a believer in art deriving its power from a primitive impulse, I expected to find Hogan vulgar but hoped he would be inventive.

Alas, he was trouncingly boring, with no idea of how to work his material. His earthiness was sheer hard-hat invective. His best line was reminiscence. Like Barry Humphries' character Sandy Stone, Hogan went in search of time past. He was quite good on, if inadvisedly proud of, the awfulness of the Australian male's sexual education, which has been such bad news for the men of my generation and even worse news for the women.

He recalled accurately how you bought your best girl scorched almonds at the pictures but fobbed off your second best with conversation lollies (they were shapes of tooth-breaking candy with messages in pink ink). Unfortunately he lacked the discrimination necessary to organise such resonant subject-matter. The linguistic fastidiousness of Humphries he just couldn't match. Hardly any Australian *can* match it, since it is linked to the consciously European richness of Humphries' personal culture. Humphries' internationalism, unlike George Lazenby's, is not an ad-man's shibboleth but a condition of mind. The force of intellect Humphries brings to the seemingly worthless minutiae of everyday Australian life depends on his studious immersion in European culture and his readiness to measure his work by its standards.

Look through the collections of Australian paintings in the Sydney and Melbourne galleries and you quickly see that for Australian artists the price of losing touch with the rest of the world is to be forced into copying the rest of the world, and that this has never been more true than recently, when arrogant self-sufficiency has resulted in the most abject plagiarism of international fashions. The strong periods of Australian painting have always depended on painters recognising the necessity for educating themselves abroad. Any Australian painter could apply European techniques to Australian subjects. What counted was applying European standards.

The pre-First World War painters did that, and to a certain extent the post-Second World War painters did too, with Sidney Nolan the most famous example. The creative self-confidence of both schools was humble at the core – the ideal order of events in an artistic personality, whatever the medium. But the young artists who received the largesse of the Whitlam regime seem to me to represent a return to insularity.

The ideology of nationalist self-sufficiency – the Australian 'renaissance' – has mainly acted as licence for provincialism, not just in painting but in films, drama and literature as well. The Australian cinema, if it can produce a few more films as good as *Picnic at Hanging Rock*, will actually be getting somewhere, after years of doing nothing except bombard British film magazines with meaningless advertisements announcing: 'Suddenly the Australians are taking over.' But it must be emphasised that *Picnic at Hanging Rock* is the exception. Scores of feature films have been made in Australia since the Whitlam Government introduced subsidies, but the average among them is unsaleable abroad and unwatchable at home. Bruce Beresford's *Barry McKenzie*, the first feature to be made under the new system, was a strong father which has had some weak progeny. Most of them have been showered with critical praise but the accolades are worthless, since they are composed by journalists devoid of standards. (Peter Weir, director of both *Picnic at Hanging Rock* and *The Cars That Ate Paris*, is the first to insist that premature canonisation is the biggest threat facing the young Australian film director today.)

It was the critical journalism which finally got me down, making me realise that my birthplace would probably have no place for me even if I decided to go back. Australia has its equivalents of the weekly magazines and posh papers which I read and write for here both as a way of life and a means to pay for it. But they are equivalents only in their format. There is plenty of good will and vigour and even talent in them but there are no consistent standards. It is not so much a lack of writing as a lack of editing. Punctilious editing is the real secret behind most of the good literary journalism done in London. Even the best of the Australian publications are full of copy which in London would be regarded as unpublishable. The literary journalist who has never been strictly blue-pencilled will never develop. And although it might be said that whether or not its literary journalism is any good is not of much importance to a young and rich country, it is of importance to me.

So one had had good reasons for sailing away, even though they did not become apparent until years later. But as I got ready to leave again, there was no mistaking the attractiveness of what was being left behind. On the last day of my trip I lunched with my family at Doyle's, the superb fish restaurant at Watson's Bay on Sydney Harbour. Sitting shirtless in the bright sun with the ultra-violet eating into my skin which had once never been white and now would never again be really brown, I ate feathery prawn cutlets and succulent whiting fillets while the children played naked amongst the beached boats and under the wharves. The fish – caught on a hand line and iced in the boat – were symphonic. Looking up-harbour towards the Bridge, you could see yachts and hydrofoils racing on the crushed diamond water, while container ships being tugged for the sea were giant cut-outs in the dazzle. Life seemed very close to God.

Perhaps that's the real reason for leaving: that Paradise on Earth leaves you nothing to achieve. But it's possible to make too much of artistic self-exile. Twenty-four hours after leaving Sydney I was back in London. The journey which once took me five weeks and felt irreversible now takes a day and feels like nothing except a bad night's sleep.

June 27, 1976

Footnote Eight years later I would have tried to sound more grateful for the hearteningly many high-grade Australian films. But the general point remains true: the average Australian film is not *The Getting of Wisdom* but *Goodbye Paradise*.

Postcard from Russia

THE MOST exciting way of getting into Russia is to cross Germany in a sealed train and arrive at the Finland Station in St Petersburg to be greeted by a cheering revolutionary mob who promptly rename the city after you. This approach being no longer possible, the next best method is to book a Sovereign package tour through British Airways, thereby ensuring that there will be none of that humdrum business about stepping on and off aircraft at the appointed time. It was an exciting few days our tiny band had of it, waiting to see which flight we would be rebooked on, if any. Finally it was Aeroflot that assumed the burden of taking us to our week of adventure behind the Iron Curtain.

Kicked by the 92,000 horses of its four Kuznetsov KN-8-4 turbofans our half-empty Ilyushin Il-62 scrambled out of Heathrow like a MiG-21. The cabin smelled of kerosene and was colder than a three-star freezer but not to worry, because in less time than it took to recover from the meal provided (packaged in London, it was to be our last contact with the West) we were on Soviet soil at Sheremetsevo airport,

Moscow. Valentina, our Intourist guide, had come to meet us. There were a dozen of us and only one of her, but she was the duck and we were the ducklings. Wherever she cruised, we paddled energetically in her wake.

Arriving at the Metropole Hotel late in the evening, we paddled straight into the past. The Metropole is bang in the centre of the city and, like every other good-looking building in the Soviet Union, dates from before the Revolution. By Western standards it's a flea-trap, but at least it's an atmospheric flea-trap, retaining all its original cherubs, chandeliers and stained glass. To the Muscovites the place is simply Dreamsville. We found the ballroom full of them, all dancing frantically to 'Heart of my Heart', played by a six-piece combo in which the clarinet had been heavily influenced by Benny Goodman. Bouncing off each other like dodgems, the dancing couples each consisted of (a) a brutally barbered man doing the steering and (b) a strapping wench providing the power. All dolled up in their Saturday-night best, the girls were culture-shock incarnate. Their clothes were straight from Oxfam and their coiffures seemed to have been created by a blacklisted Hollywood hairstylist who had taken to drink and gone blind.

At this point I shall give up any attempt at chronological presentation and take refuge in the 'blur of impressions' technique, leading off with the blurred impression that women's hairstyles play a large part in the Soviet economy. There is a hairstyle parlour in every block and a hairstyle under the helmet of every lady construction worker. It might not be much of a hairstyle, but it's a brave try, and helps distract attention from the clothes, which are amazing.

It's not just a matter of few women being able to afford to dress well: there is nothing good to buy even if they save up the money. The trouser suits in the window of GUM, the big Moscow department store beside Red Square, don't just cost more than £100 at the official exchange rate, they look like Hell. At the more ambitious shops on Kuznetsky Bridge, the once-famous fashion street behind the Bolshoi, the clothes are twice as expensive again but no less hideous. There is a special poignancy about Kuznetsky Bridge, because in Pushkin's time it was much satirised by the literary men as the place where the fine young ladies who broke their hearts went to buy French fripperies. The shops are as they were, but there is nothing in them.

In the official logic of Soviet life, essentials come cheap and luxuries come dear. But the facts say that luxuries hardly come at all. The queues you see everywhere are mainly for things that aren't yet in stock but soon might be. A pair of women's tights costs £9 plus and has to be imported from East Germany, which for the Soviet Union counts as Babylon.

But the German tights got through. The German tanks didn't. There are huge memorials outside Moscow and Leningrad to mark the places where the *Wehrmacht* was stopped cold, literally frozen in its tracks. For any visiting liberal, the central fact of Soviet history very properly remains the war waged by the Soviet Government against the liberty, and in millions of cases the lives, of its own people. But for Russians the central fact is the war waged against Nazi Germany. The 10 million slain by Stalin are at best a subject of rumour, since the flow of information which started during the Thaw has by now frozen up again. But the 20 million lost in the Second World War are a vivid memory. If, as seems likely, steps have been taken to ensure that nobody else will ever be able to assume the unchallenged power wielded by Stalin, it could have less to do with his purges than with his blunders. By weakening the officer corps at a crucial stage and refusing to heed advice, he very nearly lost his people the war.

On this subject if on no other, a modicum of sincere feeling infuses the official propaganda. Certainly the regime is lying when it blames the war, rather than its own rigidity, for the continued bleakness of Soviet life. But both powerful and powerless are of one mind in their determination never to be invaded again. On the Tomb of the Unknown Warrior outside the Kremlin wall the inscription reads: 'Your name is unknown but your death is immortal.' Touchingly, it is in the familiar form, as if addressed to a son. Old ladies leave flowers and cry.

The same old ladies queue for Lenin's tomb, but that's another issue. Even older ladies linger outside the few remaining active churches. It's a matter of faith, the Leninist faith having the merit that its propagation receives a whopping slice of the State budget, while Christianity is left to die of neglect. Since a visit to Lenin's waxwork was not on our schedule, I contented myself with paddling away from Valentina and taking a hinge at the Lenin Museum, just at the entrance to Red Square. This I can recommend, even though all the inscriptions are in Russian. Brilliantly laid out, the place is bung full of Leninalia – including his black Rolls-Royce – and helps give you an idea of what happens when a man is worshipped as a God. Hagiolatry turns to halitosis.

There are two main advantages in learning a few words of Russian before you make the trip. The first advantage is that the Russians, like the Italians (and unlike the French), respond warmly to the merest attempt at saying some little thing in their language. When, after consulting my pocket dictionary, I told the floor superintendent that the light bulb in my bathroom was burned out (actually I said, 'The bath illumination have been destroyed,' but let that pass), she and her assistant burst into applause, whereupon a team of ladies in blue overalls sprinted down the corridor and fixed the thing in nothing flat.

The second advantage is that you will not be so easily fooled by the suggestion that the Soviet Union is Arcadia made actual. What has been made actual in the Soviet Union is boredom. Having discovered that boring the people works better than killing them, the State has gone on being boring for so long that it has ended up by boring even itself. It is true that the people do not litter the streets or write graffiti on the walls. They don't need to: the Government does it for them. There are posters and banners absolutely everywhere.

Chesterton said that Times Square in New York would look like paradise to anyone who couldn't read. The Russian alphabet looks very decorative to anyone who can't understand it. But if you can puzzle out what all those gigantic inscriptions are saying, you gradually realise that every major building in Moscow and Leningrad is engaged full-time in boring the public witless.

It was reasonably jolly to discover that the huge words on top of the power station in Moscow were a famous quotation from Lenin: COMMUNISM IS SOVIET POWER PLUS THE ELECTRIFICATION OF THE ENTIRE COUNTRY. But the slogan on top of the Metropole was less digestible: RAISE HIGH THE BANNER OF PRO-LETARIAN INTERNATIONALISM! Nine out of every ten slogans finish with an exclamation mark. Since the Soviet Union is currently in the throes of assimilating the directives handed down by the XXVth Party Congress, the same general invitation is repeated every few yards: LET US FULFIL THE DECISIONS OF THE XXVth PARTY CONGRESS! The decisions filled the whole front page of *Pravda*. There were hundreds of them. Without exception they finished with an exclamation mark.

While we were there, Lenin's 107th birthday fell due. The paper *Soviet Russia*, mouthpiece of the Central Committee, carried the full text of a heroically tedious speech made to the Praesidium by ideologist M.B. Zumyanin, marking the occasion. Marking it flat. Under a half-page photo of the Praesidium, sitting beneath the inevitable portrait of Lenin, the caption informs us that we are looking at 'a triumphant meeting of the Praesidium, dedicated to the 107th anniversary of the birthday of V.I. Lenin'. There follows the headline: LENINISM – REVOLUTIONARY BANNER OF OUR EPOCH. A sub-heading informs us that we are about to read a speech given 'in a triumphant meeting in Moscow, dedicated to the 107th anniversary of the birthday of V.I. Lenin'. This introduces the speech proper, running from page one to page three in small print. It begins:

35

'Comrades! One hundred and seven years after the birthday of Vladimir Ilyich Lenin . . .' You get the drift. Actually this was the speech the Chinese delegate walked out of, but surely not because of its veiled criticisms of China. He just saw his chance and split.

The cult of Brezhnev is low-temperature compared with what used to be turned on for Stalin. Brezhnev's thoughts are everywhere, but the letters are seldom more than six feet high. In *Pravda* there are always scores of references to his latest speech, in which he always declares himself to be against Imperialism and for Peace. His name is invariably given as General Secretary of the Central Committee of the Communist Party Comrade Brezhnev. But there aren't many shrines to him that can't be easily dismantled: Brezhnev could be made to vanish from the landscape as completely as Khrushchev, who is not even buried with all the other Party heroes in the Kremlin wall. (He's over in the Nunnery, in a part of the graveyard we couldn't visit.) Stalin is still in the wall, but he'll never get back into Lenin's tomb, where he lay for the short period of his immortality. Lenin is the only deity allowed at the moment.

And one's enough. Any building he isn't on, he's in. There is a hulking bust of him inside Moscow's Leningrad Station, and when you get off the train at the other end you find an equally hulking bust inside Leningrad's Moscow Station. But from the outside the stations look exactly the same as they did when Anna Karenina fell under her train. On the whole the Soviet Union has done a good job of preserving the pre-revolutionary artistic heritage. Since there is hardly any such thing as a *post*-revolutionary artistic heritage you might say that it was the least they could do, but considering the aristocratic and/or bourgeois provenance of what they inherited, they have been remarkably tolerant in looking after it. (For anything untoward produced after 1917, I need hardly point out, there is no tolerance available at all.)

The Tsars' summer palaces outside Leningrad were severely damaged by the occupying *Wehrmacht* but they have been painstakingly reassembled. The Russian rococo is the most human of all grand styles, never getting out of scale with the people inside it. It went on exuding the formative intelligence of Peter the Great long after the Russian royal family had declined into mediocrity. The supreme example, in Leningrad itself, is, of course, the Winter Palace, now merely the largest of the several buildings which form the Hermitage.

The paintings in the Hermitage would alone constitute sufficient reason for visiting the USSR. Nina, our Intourist guide in Leningrad, knew a lot about painting, but she was allowed to conduct only one official tour of the Hermitage. You need three or four visits to get to grips with the place, so I recommend paddling off. The Imperial collections drip with masterpieces – Leonardos, Giorgiones, Rembrandts, a Michelangelo statue, etc. – but more remarkable still are the rooms full of French paintings bought at the turn of this century more or less straight off the easel. A wall of Bonnards, a room full of Cézannes, another room full of Rose, Blue and early Cubist Picassos – it's unbelievable. (The equivalent rooms in Moscow's Pushkin Museum are unbelievable too.) Such purchasing was only one aspect of the rich, bourgeois culture which otherwise gave rise to Diaghilev, and which the Revolution cut down in full flower.

There is a room entirely devoted to a staggering collection of Gauguins. Looking down from a window of this room into the square below – the square to which the people once came asking for bread and got bullets in reply – I could see the flagstones being torn up to make way for a mosaic hailing the sixtieth anniversary of the Revolution, which will be celebrated next November (i.e., October, old-style) and will be a very big deal. There are no prizes for guessing whose face will feature in the mosaic.

As we now know, the artistic euphoria of the decade after the Revolution was a false dawn. Night descended in 1917 and the sun has never really re-arisen. Only in music – and barely even in that, when you compare the fruitfulness of the nineteenth century – has creativity been allowed to continue. In a way this is lucky for us, because there can't be much doubt that Russian culture would have overwhelmed the world. It took the Revolution to stop it.

Our package tour included a good seat in Moscow's Congress Palace (the very place from which the Chinese delegate sloped out a few days later) for the Siberian Folk Dance Ensemble. It was a big kick to be sitting in the Kremlin surrounded by Mongolian generals covered with decorations, but the folk dancing itself was tedium epitomised. The packed house of 5,000 people all pretended to be having a marvellous time but there was no avoiding the conclusion that here was culture less ethnic than embalmed – the whole deal was as stiff as Lenin's corpse.

In Leningrad we went to the circus, which was a better bet, but once again I advise paddling away and asking your hotel's Service Bureau to book you into as many operas and ballets as you have spare nights to fill. Stick to the old stuff if you want to be entertained and try something modern if you want to see how far Russian art has gone down the tubes. At the Kirov there was a modern ballet called *Till Eulenspiegel*. The music was composed not by Richard Strauss but by People's Artist E.A. Glebova. It was loudly inane. The libretto and choreography were both by Honoured Artistic Worker V.N. Elizarev. They were pretentious and trite respectively. The subject was the triumph of Freedom and Love over Fascism. The décor and costumes seemed to have been provided by GUM. The dancing was a muffled echo of Martha Graham. Flexing his powerful bottom, Freedom did arabesques while Love used him as a divan and Fascism writhed menacingly in the background. The total effect was of a Western avant-garde production *circa* 1957, but really it was all even older hat than that.

Just around the corner from our hotel (the Evropaeska – all the same cherubs as the Metropole) the Maly Theatre gave Prokofiev's *Romeo and Juliet*, with new choreography by O.M. Vinogradov. This was more like it, the music being hard not to respond to, but even here the dancing was largely a waste of energy. Perhaps I was prejudiced, seated as I was behind a lady whose upswept hairstyle – which gradually came apart as the evening wore on – suggested that she had surfaced abruptly underneath a heron's nest. But from what I could see through the cloud of wisps and strands, Romeo and Juliet danced like Rodnina and Zaitsev minus the skates. Bundles of athleticism but little emotional tact. It is all very well to argue that opera and ballet deal with emotions rather than ideas, but if ideas are not allowed to exist then there is nothing left with which to think about emotions.

Valentina and Nina both love their country but would like to visit the West. God knows what they will think of it – I can see how it is bound to shock them. Packing for home, however, I was glad enough to be going back. A blur of impressions should always end with 'a personal note', so let me say that I had thought the equality which supposedly prevails in the Soviet Union would appeal to my levelling Australian spirit. In a way it does, but the price is too high. For anyone who values the free play of the mind, inequality will always be obscene. But to extirpate both inequality *and* mind is to kill the tree along with the mistletoe.

For all its monolithic sense of purpose, the Soviet Union seems hopelessly barren when compared with the West, which has more to be said for it than we commonly allow. For example, it has the continuous excitement provided by British Airways, who sent word to Moscow that they couldn't get an aircraft any closer to us than Copenhagen. Could we meet them there? For a while it looked as if we might have to walk, but finally we got a lift in a Pan Am Boeing 707 shuttling through from Tokyo. The further West we flew the better I felt. I felt better about my own activities: in a land which allows no mocking voices, no other kind of voice sounds convincing either. I felt better about poor troubled Britain. I felt warm towards Sovereign Tours. I even felt fond of British Airways – which was bloody

generous of me, because when we got to Copenhagen it
turned out that they had gone to Amsterdam.

May 15, 1977

Postcard from New York

A s my Pan Am Boeing 747 Clipper Bald Eagle lined up to
land at Kennedy airport, it passed over a graveyard that
would have been just the right size, had it not already been
full, to bury the consequences if the pilot made a mistake.
He didn't, but as we rolled to a halt my paranoia was
undiminished. There is an old Jules Feiffer comic strip,
dating from the Fifties, in which an agonised beatnik takes a
dozen frames to tell his girlfriend the shameful truth – that he
has never been to Europe. My own shame was identical, only
in reverse. In a state of advanced, inoperable middle age, I
had never been to New York.

Had I left it too late? Nameless fears haunted the mind.
Some of them were not so nameless. One of them was called
Son of Sam. A killer was loose in New York, blasting people
from point-blank range with a .44 pistol. He had seen the
same Clint Eastwood movies as I had, but they had taken
him a different way. Would he find me? Would I get mugged?
And why was breathing so difficult? I had known it would be
hot in August, but was it supposed to be *this* hot? The air was
like chicken broth. Grease bubbles swam in it, and small
bones.

Into a Manhattan still traumatised by blackout and looting I moved at what seemed like 100 m.p.h. in the back of a

cab. The back was separated from the front by armoured glass, just as in *Taxi Driver*. Not good for the paranoia. As I was soon to learn, New York traffic seems to move at a dizzy pace for two reasons: (a) because it moves at a dizzy pace, and (b) because the cars are built low to the ground. A speed that would seem merely ill-advised in a London taxi feels like drag-racing in a New York cab piloted by a man who has modelled the back of his head on Robert De Niro and his driving style on Mario Andretti.

Suddenly the Brooklyn Bridge loomed from the dusk before my startled eyes, looking exactly as it had when Johnny Weissmuller dived off it in *Tarzan's New York Adventure*. The tall buildings of the downtown financial district climbed on the left, rope-tricks of light. The twin towers of the Trade Center were just beyond them: boxed constellations. Uptown on the right, in the north, I could see the Empire State Building, and that art deco concoction must be the Chrysler building: absurdly familiar.

To get uptown we first had to go through the Bowery, which confirmed my worst fears. Drunks who had obviously spent years dosing themselves with low-grade gasoline lurched forward mouthing pitiful offers to clean the windshield. Mario De Niro scattered them like chaff. Lady ragpickers who had devoted their lives to putting on clothes without ever taking them off shouted dementedly, as well they might, since it was about 90°F even after sunset and most of them had on so many sweaters they were unable to fall over. The squalor was paralysing. I arrived at the Algonquin vowing never to re-emerge until my week was up.

But curiosity got the better of nerves, even if it never stilled them. I ended up by loving New York, for all the corny reasons: Pace of Life, Energy, Creativity, etc. But not all of the bad vibes entirely dissipated and some of them are reverberating still in the shocked memory. For one thing, there are an awful lot of Crazies around. Some of the Crazies just quietly mumble. But most of the Crazies shout.

Where I used to live in Islington there was a deranged

virago who was famous for yelling angry obscenities. In New York she would pass unnoticed. Taking a bus downtown to Greenwich Village I was petrified to discover the automatic doors opening to admit the most insane-looking lady I have ever seen. She was like one of those women Jack Davis used to draw for *Mad* magazine, with an enormous shapeless body, basketball shoes and a few pointed teeth spaced several inches apart in the gaping maw. She sat down on two seats and immediately started bellowing: 'Ya safer up here on a bus! Ya *safer* up here than down there in the fuckn subway, right? *Because everybody's fuckn crazy down there, right? AM I FUCKN RIGHT?*'

To define the New York subway as a place where such a lady feels herself threatened might seem far-fetched, but there is plenty of evidence that it is a bad scene down there. I visited the subway car-barn on the waterfront at the north-west tip of the island, just to take a look at all the graffiti that Norman Mailer raves about. An awe-inspiring display: ego from the aerosol. One artist has taken a whole subway car to sign his name. In purple-starred gold letters as high as itself the car shouts a single word – MITCH.

But you can admire the inspired doodling of the subway's amateur decorators without being eager to ride in the results. On the day I arrived, the city took a momentary break from talking about Son of Sam in order to give fleeting attention to some unknown killer who had stabbed a lady Spanish teacher twelve times in a subway station near Lincoln Center. She had gone there to book a concert ticket. This was one of the several topics I raised with the beautiful young actress Andrea Marcovici when I took her to lunch in the Algonquin's famous Rose Room.

It was in the Rose Room that the legendary Vicious Circle used to meet and trade witticisms – Dorothy Parker, Robert Benchley and the rest. It was in the Rose Room, today still as celebrity-packed as it ever was, that your reporter wined and dined Miss Marcovici, who first sprang to notice in the film *The Front* and in October will star as Nefertiti in a zillion-dollar Broadway musical. The killer, she told me firmly, had undoubtedly known the victim personally. A visitor was perfectly safe in New York.

Young, beautiful and strong-minded, Miss Marcovici made me feel old, jaded and overweight. Not yet fully famous but plainly on her way up, she had more than enough cachet to raise my stock at the Algonquin a mile. After my dazzling companion had swept out, the *maître d'hôtel* and the bell-captain wanted to know my secret. 'Dat's de guy whut wuz in here wit' Angela Muggervoochie,' whispered one porter to another. In New York everybody wants to be somebody. If you aren't somebody yourself, knowing somebody helps. For the rest of my stay I bathed in reflected glory.

The bigger the heap, the more people there must be who are not at the top of it. Life at the bottom in New York looks vividly nasty. You don't have to have Son of Sam after you to feel deprived. When the lights went out, Manhattan turned into two different cities, the one that behaved itself and the one that didn't. Law-abiding New Yorkers were shocked by the looting, but few of them saw it. They only read about it. Territories are sealed off from one another by invisible fields of force – one end of a street can be safe and the other end not. Bordered by haves on the East Side and have-nots on the West, Central Park is safe by day, dangerous by night.

But more New Yorkers live outside Manhattan than inside it. Brooklyn, sometimes called Manhattan's bedroom, would be the fourth largest city in the country even if the rest of New York did not exist – three million people live there. They get more peace and quiet than most of the inhabitants of Manhattan. (Certainly they do better than anyone in the South Bronx, which is currently being burned down – some say by children, some say for the insurance, some say both.) Yet for all but the wealthiest, the restful life is hard to obtain in New York. For the professional classes the thing to do is commute.

I visited one indefatigable commuter: Pauline Kael, the *New Yorker*'s justly celebrated film critic. She lives in Stockbridge in Massachusetts. Instructions arrived at the

43

Algonquin telling me how to get there. A 100 m.p.h. cab to La Guardia airport. Then a tiny twin-engined Beechcraft airliner for a one-hour trip to the Berkshires. We flew through a storm all the way. Lighting his cigarette one-handed, the pilot did a no-sweat Buzz Sawyer routine while his co-pilot made a great show of understanding the map. The aircraft behaved like a pair of underpants in a washing machine. Nonchalant, I occupied the time by reading. I was reading the safety leaflet, but at least I was trying: New Yorkers are strong on cool. As we raced the rain towards the ground, it was becoming clear to me where Miss Kael gets the toughness of her prose style. Just making it to the office every week must hone her nerve like a hunting-knife.

In the Berkshires I was taken to Tanglewood, Music Inn and Alice's Restaurant, where we ate a superb omelette and met Alice. I got to meet Alice because I was the guy with Pauline Kael. Reflected glory. These are the places forever associated, in the minds of my jazz-reared generation, with the MJQ, Sonny Rollins and Jimmy Giuffre. I heard a beautiful saxophone as I passed the door of a bar. I opened the door. It was Jimmy Giuffre.

The pilot climbed aboard after burning incense to his ancestors, and as the diminutive figure of Miss Kael waved bravely in the prop-wash I headed back to New York think-ing that I had seen the good life – to live in the loveliest of all countrysides and work in the most stimulating of all cities. If you're doing very well indeed, of course, you can have it both ways without moving off Manhattan. Stephen Sondheim, for example.

I called on Sondheim at his house in the East Side of midtown Manhattan – a fashionable district where a quarter of a million dollars down plus crippling rates will buy you the chance to live within spitting distance of Truman Capote. Here Sondheim lives with his mind-boggling record collec-tion and the knowledge, which would drive a less self-questioning spirit to the sin of pride, that he is by now universally regarded as the lyric poet of latterday New York.

Sondheim's house has a back garden, joining up with the back gardens of the other houses on the block to form a sheltered square of greenery. It is a common enough arrangement in London. Here it costs a fortune. Katharine Hepburn lives next door. Only the householders can roam in the vegetation. I asked Sondheim if Son of Sam could get in. The answer was that he would have to buy a house.

Son of Sam was arrested the next morning. The New York *Post* gave the impression that it had more or less brought off the coup all by itself. 'CAUGHT!' it screamed. The *Post* is owned by my compatriot Rupert Murdoch. All week long it had been running an artist's impression of Son of Sam. When Son of Sam was finally arrested, other newspapers were not slow to point out that he looked nothing like the artist's impression. Undaunted, the *Post* ran Son of Sam's photograph beside the artist's impression, defiantly instructing its readership to 'compare the sketch and the man'. The sketch looked more like Rupert Murdoch than it looked like Son of Sam.

Owning the New York *Post* has given Murdoch the chance to do what he is best at – making life sound like a bad movie. For endless weeks, as the *Post* played detective, it was like Dana Andrews and Ida Lupino on the trail of the Lipstick Killer. A better technique for encouraging copycat crimes couldn't be devised. The *New Yorker*, from its dusty offices – I visited them and measured the dust on your behalf – has dustily told Murdoch where he gets off. He won't get off: he's selling papers. The *New York Times* is standing on its dignity and adding a new supplement for every day of the week with the prospect that the weekday editions will end up weighing as much as the notoriously massive Sunday edition. (It is on record that once upon a time the Sunday edition, air-dropped to a subscriber in Texas, killed a cow.)

Profiting from the momentary hiatus between Son of Sam's arrest and the inevitable advent of Grandson of Sam, I walked that evening to the Music Box theatre and paid $15 to see *Side by Side by Sondheim*. Broadway theatre tickets are expensive (although in other respects London has become just as costly as New York) but in this case it was money well spent. New York potentiates music the same way that alcohol potentiates certain pills. Old hits by the Lovin' Spoonful sound richer than ever when they pour from your radio on a hot night. On a cross-town bus from the 42nd Street pier to the United Nations I passed a black gospel revival choir singing in a car park. The electric guitars set the whole bus dancing. 42nd Street! And somehow Sondheim, with his vast, unforced scholarship in both music and lyrics, has got all that into his songs. The show is a smash hit. Presenting it, Ned Sherrin is on top of the world. So guess who I took to dinner at the Algonquin?

As Sherrin tucked into the steak tartare, I put to him Miss Marcovici's proposition that the Spanish teacher had been murdered by someone who knew her. Munching elegantly, Sherrin agreed that this was statistically probable. Official Police Department figures showed that murders of strangers by strangers were decreasing, while murders of acquaintances by acquaintances were increasing all the time. 'One concludes', Sherrin summed up, 'that New York is becoming a friendlier place.' Having been seen in the company of Ned Sherrin, Broadway star, my prestige in the hotel was enhanced even further. 'Remember the guy what wus wit' Anthea Magnavootl? Tonight he wus wit' Ed Sherman.'

As a city, New York is broke and seems determined to stay that way. There is not much that the people can feel they own. Even the great art museums – the Metropolitan, the Guggenheim, the Museum of Modern Art – constantly remind them of what they owe to private benefaction. But irritation is easily allayed, when you are regaled with the lyrical wit of the Klee exhibition currently running at the Guggenheim; or the Picasso etchings at the Museum of Modern Art; or the retina-searing riches of the Metropolitan. The best museum of all is the Frick Collection, where you can contemplate the Vermeers and the Memlings to the restrained music of a fountain burbling in the courtyard. Peace, quiet and civilisation – it took a multi-millionaire steel baron to buy them for the people. The city could never have raised the scratch.

Everything I had ever heard about American hospitality turned out to be true. Nor is it an empty gesture, since it costs time. In New York time is money and money burns. If your car is towed away it will cost you $25 for the traffic violation, $65 for the towing fee and $5 a day for every day the car is in the pound. People wait for the police auction and buy their cars back, or else just forget about them. In New York there is not much that can't be thrown away – including, alas, people. Grand Central Station was saved by public outcry but public outcry is a fickle jade.

The city is infinitely mutable. Looking back on it from the Staten Island ferry on a rainy day, you can see it dissolving in the clouds. The island Peter Minuit conned out of the Indians is more substantial than what has been put on top of it. The rock removed to make way for the foundations of the Empire State Building weighed more than the building.

Leaving from Kennedy, I marvelled all over again at a city that could so blithely discard the airport's original, beautiful name – Idlewild. Nor could I ever be quite comfortable in a town where the index of all achievement is to have your name in lights. Lights can be switched off. But a whole week after leaving New York I am still high as a kite on adrenalin. Even in the hottest, flattest month of the year, so much happened so fast.

I even got mugged. At the corner of 44th and Broadway, just off Times Square, I was pinned against a wall by a black as big as Woody Strode. My life flashed by between my eyes and his belt-buckle. I had only $75 on me – how could that be enough to appease his ethnic fury? His hand closed around my shoulder. This was it. 'Hey, man,' he growled, 'I hate to ask you this, but can you loan me 25 cents for a hot-dog?'

August 28, 1978

Postcard from Japan

1 An Exchange of Views

BY COURTESY of a British Airways Boeing 707 I was crossing in a few hours the same distance that cost Marco
Polo years of his life, but the speed of modern travel has its
penalties. Among these had been the in-flight movie, which I
dimly remember was about bears playing baseball.

From the air Siberia looks like cold nothing. The Sea of
Japan looks like wet nothing. But Japan itself, at your first
glimpse of it, looks like something. Even geographically it's a
busy place.

Immediately you are impressed by the wealth of detail – an
impression that will never leave you for as long as you are
there. Only a tenth of the land is useful for anything. The
remaining nine-tenths, when you look down on it, is a kind of
corduroy velvet: country so precipitously convoluted that the
rivers flowing through it look like the silver trails of inebri-
ated slugs. The useful tenth is inhabited, cultivated and
industrialised with an intensity that boggles the Occidental
mind. I had never seen anything like it in my life.

Seen from high up, the basic agricultural pattern of the
Western countries is of accumulated squares. America looks
like a patchwork quilt; France like another quilt but with
smaller patches; Britain like yet another quilt with smaller
patches still. The basic agricultural pattern of Japan is
of proliferating brain cells. Everywhere a rice paddy can
possibly be put a rice paddy has been put, even if it is only the
size of a table napkin.

Merging with this nervous tissue, like bionic grafts, are the
areas of urban habitation and industry. One hundred and

48

ten million people live and work down there, most of them in conurbations which to the stratospheric eye look like infinitely elaborate printed circuits. You can tell straight away, before you even touch the ground, that in Japan there is nowhere anybody can hide. They're all in it together.

When the plane starts to land at Tokyo's Haneda airport one tends to panic slightly because from the tilting window the built-up area seems to go on for ever, with no edge except the sea. Later experience confirms the truth of this suspicion – Tokyo is really just a name for one of the more drastically overpopulated districts in a single, enormous city that goes on and on for hundreds of miles – but for the moment the panic is cancelled out by the more immediate fear that one is about to land in an oil refinery.

The plane comes in low over Tokyo Bay and touches down at a point where the water abruptly becomes concrete, with a plenitude of industrial capacity looming on all sides. The sheer crowdedness of Japan is already happening even at the airport – a place which in the next few hours I was to see a lot of, because I had neglected to provide myself with a visa. Even after sixteen years in Britain I still carry an Australian passport, and although Britain has a no-visa arrangement with Japan, Australia hasn't.

Half a day of negotiations provided eloquent proof that in Japan subsequent action may be swift but the preliminary formalities must always be thorough. The smiling but inexorable lady immigration official did everything except interrogate separate parts of my body to make sure that they belonged to the same person. Documents were produced on which I had to fill out details of the *Observer*'s ownership, management structure, circulation and history over 200 years. By this time I was getting worried about being deported straight back to London with nothing to show for the trip except a very short article.

The situation was saved by the arrival of a public relations officer from JETRO – the government-sponsored trade organisation who were my hosts for the visit. A young man of awesome patience and efficiency, Mr Jun Tsunekawa was to be my Virgil for the entire junket. In Japan there is really no such thing as first-name terms, so even when we got to know each other well we always remained Mr James and Mr Tsunekawa. But in my mind he was known straight away and for ever as Jun-san the PR-man.

After filling out several hundred forms on his own account, making a few score phone calls and helping me to suspend the immigration lady's disbelief in the existence of the Atlantic Richfield Company, Jun-san finally sprang me from the trap. We fell into a taxi and headed for central Tokyo. During the rush-hour Tokyo's millions of cars form a traffic-jam which lacks a glacier's sole virtue – movement. But this was merely the middle afternoon, so the taxi-drivers on the flyovers were free to express themselves. The old joke says that in the kamikaze squadrons the failures were the ones who came back. The old joke forgets to mention that they're all driving taxis in Tokyo.

The Imperial Hotel is a few yards from the Ginza in one direction and the Imperial Palace in another. The old Imperial was one of Frank Lloyd Wright's masterpieces and was reckoned to be full of character if you didn't mind getting down on your hands and knees to look through the window. The new Imperial has nothing quirky about it except a standard of service that is little short of uncanny. Platoons of highly motivated staff are poised in the starting blocks ready to anticipate your every wish. If they can't read your mind and supply what you want before you ask for it, they hold themselves to have failed.

I later learned that a high standard of service is general throughout Japan, but for the moment it seemed an emollient specifically laid on by the fates to console me for the visa blunder, which had wiped out the time allotted for visiting the Sony factory. Jun-san had worked out a jam-packed itinerary which left no room for errors but on this one occasion there was nothing to be done. The Sony visit was out, and very soon Mr James was out too – out cold. While

Jun-san commuted back to his wife and children, I turned on the Hitachi TV set and fell into a jet-lag sleep while sitting upright in bed watching Samurai running at one another with little swords.

That was the last quiet moment. For the next eleven days the pace was a cracker. In England JETRO had asked me to supply a list of things I wanted to see. Assuming they would make a limited choice according to what was available or convenient, I had asked to look at everything from heavy industry to flower arrangement. I now learned to my horror that they had taken the whole thing literally and had put together a programme involving half a dozen big cities, most of the important shrines and temples, tours of factories, visits to pearl farms, and a night in a traditional inn. All these things were to be joined up by rides in the Bullet Train, which would transport us at a steady 120 m.p.h. on the rare occasions when we were not doing something else.

First there would be conferences, meetings, lunches and dinners in Tokyo, with the object of providing opportunities to Exchange Views. In Japan it is always called an Exchange of Views, even when the only view that matters is theirs. The more anxious they are to tell you something, the more polite they get – and at that moment they were very anxious to tell us something, so the politeness was overwhelming.

For the next two days I was ushered from conference room to conference room. A team of Japanese officials would be waiting in each room, the older men of unnervingly high rank, the younger men of vibrantly keen demeanour. One and all were dressed in impeccable taste. Having been warned in advance that it was suit and tie all the way, I had brought both my suit and my tie, but in this company there was no hope of looking anything except seedy. They didn't seem to mind. They Exchanged Views undaunted.

Always deferring to their seniors, the youngsters made the points. Every point was backed up with Xeroxed graphs and figures, until my briefcase started looking like a kitbag. I am so far from being an economist that I have always admired

Sir Alec Douglas-Home for knowing which matches to move, but gradually a picture emerged that even I could understand.

Japan's balance of payments surplus has grown so big as to become embarrassing. Unless something is done to reduce it, tariff barriers might be put up in the countries to which Japan exports. But Japan can't afford to export less, since she is already in a recession. Therefore she will have to import more.

It is not easy for foreign countries to trade in the Japanese market, but America has done well, there is a demand for high-quality British goods, and there is no reason why everybody should not do better, especially with encouragement and advice from the Japanese Government. In other words, it's open house.

Though I never, then or subsequently, conquered the suspicion that they had chosen the wrong man to entrust with their message, still I was impressed with their sincerity. After the frightening success at selling things to the rest of the world, the Japanese now really and truly want the rest of the world to sell things to them. One catch, however, had already become obvious even to my inexpert eye. It takes only a few hours in Tokyo to make you wonder whether there is anything in the way of consumer goods that Japan doesn't make better and cheaper than anybody else.

The cars that choke the streets are not only all new, they are solidly made: the days are past when shortage of materials enforced shoddiness of construction. On the footpaths, the population is well dressed. You would expect the Japanese to make their traditional clothes well, but they make Western clothes well too. The men's suits are beautifully cut, and even the more humble of the women wear soft fabrics in a subtle range of colours – always a sign of wealth in Britain and America, and in Russia totally unknown.

Japanese shed no litter. (Nor is the city air any longer polluted – the only reason that you see some people wearing gauze masks is that it is considered bad manners to give other people your cold.) But they are not just spick and span. They are tasteful in a way that unites the past with the present and the higher orders with the lower. You never get the sense, as you do in most other countries, that the upper classes have the monopoly of aesthetic gratification.

That much you can see on the streets and footpaths. Then, when you go inside the shops, you start seeing the consumer goods – another revelation. In a discount house for electric appliances Jun-san and his raffish colleague Mr Sato (who daringly wore no tie) showed me a new-model pocket calculator. I bought it for about £8 and have it before me on my desk as I write. It runs on a lithium battery and has about the same dimensions, including thickness, as a rye crispbread. A country that can make something like that can make anything.

But before I had time to get doubtful about our chances of further penetrating the new Japan, Jun-san whisked me into the old. The road west from Tokyo to Kyoto is called the Tokaido. In Hiroshige's time the 300 or so miles was a fortnight's brisk walk, although he himself took longer, since he was sketching for the famous series of woodcuts with which he finally toppled Hokusai from popularity.

Nowadays you travel up and down the Tokaido on the *Shinkansen*, known to the world as the Bullet Train. (*Shinkansen* really just means New Line, but the world wants romance.) The *Shinkansen* moves at about the same speed as BR's 125 but nothing stops it except an earthquake. After half an hour of going hell for leather it all seems very natural and you are left with nothing to do except wonder vaguely when Tokyo is going to end. It never really does: it just changes names. At one of these names, Nagoya, we got off and switched to a private line, the Kinki Nippon Railway, which took us into the Ise peninsula, where the shrines and pearls are.

For the next few days, by dint of the Kinki Nippon and a succession of limousines laid on by JETRO, we zigzagged around the peninsula absorbing the surprisingly large amounts of old Japan which still remain carefully preserved among the factories and ricefields. A measure of the holiness of the Buddhist and Shinto shrines is the fact that the land inside their boundaries is used for nothing except gardens.

The Meiji restoration in 1868 brought an end to the long reign of the Tokugawa Shoguns and launched Japan into the modern era. But looking at the shrines, temples and palaces you feel that the continuity between the ancient Heian Period and the current Showa Era remains largely unbroken. For one thing the Japanese are still physically involved with the far past. The Emperor and the Prime Minister come to the great Ise shrine every year. The Emperor's white horses are kept there. Some of the Ise shrine's bleached wooden buildings are rebuilt entirely every twenty years, exactly as they were before, tile for tile, nail for nail. The substance changes but the form persists, just as there are always carp in the clear river century after century.

In Nara, which was the capital before Kyoto, which was the capital before Tokyo, I saw the world's oldest wooden building. It belongs to a Buddhist temple and dates from the seventh century. Not far away is the pavilion containing the Daibutsu, a statue of Buddha more than 60 feet high. The pavilion roof is currently being restored at a cost of five billion yen, which according to my crispbread calculator is a hell of a lot of money. Standing in the shadow of the Daibutsu's left knee, I said the only prayer of my adult life, on the principle that it would be foolish to waste the opportunity. If anyone is in touch with the man upstairs, the Daibutsu is.

In Kyoto I contemplated the famous Zen garden of stones and raked sand in the Ryuan-ji temple and walked across the stepping-stones in the lotus gardens of the Heian Shinto shrine. It was all magically lovely, but on the whole I found the secular architecture more appealing than the religious. In their bland, sweet eclecticism the shrines remind you of the rest of the East, but the buildings put up by the nobility represent a conjunction of high art and worldly power more familiar to the Western mind, which will readily find comparisons in Renaissance Florence and Petrine Russia.

The edifice not to be missed is the Nijo Castle in Kyoto. The Nijo-jo was built in 1603 by Ieyasu, the first of the Tokugawa Shoguns. Inside its stone walls the wood, cloth and paper rooms combine force with delicacy in the most astonishing way, as if the acme of taste had been reached and there was nowhere else to go. Coffered beams with gold-plated copper nail-covers mark off areas of wall exquisitely decorated with Kano murals of cherry tree branches piled with snow.

Sunlight filters through paper windows into the long, low reception rooms behind whose sliding panels the Shogun's bodyguard were concealed ready to leap into action should one of his ambassadors prove traitor. For security at night the corridors are equipped with nightingale floors: all the boards are mounted on sleeved nails so that the whole floor sings like a bird no matter how softly you tread. Thus the Tokugawa preserved their power for centuries, until the day came when they decided to let the Emperor carry the can.

The Two Views traditional inn at Toba has received many a weary traveller, but none wearier than Mr James. I was glad to descend into the traditional bath and emerge into the traditional kimono. Jun-san opened the traditional calligraphy set, prepared the traditional ink, and taught me to write my name in Japanese. Meanwhile the traditional maid in traditional dress brought us the traditional meal. Most of this was *sushi* – raw fish. The sea cucumber was like taking a bite out of a squashball but the squid was not to be sneezed at.

At last it was time to roll out the traditional bed on the *tatami*, heap it with the traditional quilts and settle down for the traditional sleepless night. I didn't get a wink, but in the morning the Pacific was outside the window, glass-calm to the horizon. As the pale dawn broke gently over the pearl farms I wondered why I felt so at ease, considering that I had never been further away from home.

June 4, 1978

55

Postcard from Japan

2 The Bridegroom of the Sea

A BACK-BREAKING sleepless night on the floor of the Two
Views traditional inn had left me sobbing with fatigue,
but the Sumo wrestlers soon restored my spirits. Not even
Jun-san the PR-man had been able to scrape up a proper
Sumo match, since it was the wrong season. But he had
obtained permission to visit a training camp in the enormous
city of Osaka, and thither we went in the early morning.

A Sumo training camp mainly consists of a metal shed
about 40 feet by 20 feet. It has to be made of metal because
when a dozen Sumo wrestlers are throwing one another
around inside it they tend to bump into the walls, and if the
walls were made of traditional materials the wrestlers would
go right through, wrecking half a suburb before they came to
rest.

The Sumo wrestlers are not especially tall, but they are
especially big. They go out rather than up. They might even
be called fat, but they have none of the awkwardness that
usually goes with fatness. They can do a sideways splits and
touch the ground in front of them with their shoulders. You
try it.

Inside the shed was a stove on which to brew seaweed tea,
some benches for the privileged spectators, and a ring of
raked sand. Each wrestler took his turn defending the ring
against all the others in succession. After a long preliminary
routine of glowering, ground-pounding, snorting and stalk-
ing, the opponents ran suddenly into each other with the
noise of colliding water-melons. Each encounter was all over
in seconds.

The idea, it transpired, is to get the other fellow's centre

56

of gravity moving in the wrong direction, whereupon his momentum carries him out of the ring. Watching this from close quarters is like sitting on the outside of a hairpin bend during a grand prix race for articulated lorries. Every few minutes one of the wrestlers hit the wall, making it reverberate like a large gong. This would evoke a good deal of comradely chortling from his colleagues, accompanied by the ritual readjustment of jock-straps. A Sumo wrestler's jock-strap is a black belt which not only goes underneath him in order to ward off instant hernia, but has to go around him a couple of times as well. It is therefore very long.

That exercise completed, there were several minutes of Zen contemplation. Then one wrestler stood against the wall while the others formed a human pyramid and ran at him. By rights his intestines should have come out of his ears, but he smiled instead. Just when I thought these were the strongest men I had ever seen, the door of the shed rolled open and a man swayed in who made the rest of them look emaciated. This was Kitanomi, the current Sumo champion of Japan. He walked with his feet about a yard apart. He stopped, looked at the others, snorted, and swayed out again. That was his training session for the morning.

Kitanomi is so famous that even the normally impassive Jun-san got excited about securing his autograph. Jun-san had purchased special sheets of white card for this purpose. Across these Kitanomi airily waved a felt-tip. The felt-tip looked like a toothpick and the signature looked like a more than usually meaningless abstract by Franz Kline, but Jun-san was well satisfied. Sipping my seaweed tea while the wrestlers went next door to embark on the epic they call lunch, I marvelled all over again at the way the Japanese can put so much formality and ritual into the smallest thing. A Sumo bout lasts about half a minute, yet a whole way of life is built around it.

Jun-san's all-powerful schedule declared that it was time to return to the modern age. On the *Shinkansen* we raced down to Hiroshima, there to spend the morning at the Mitsubishi shipyards. Only a small part of the Mitsubishi empire, these are awe-inspiring in their size and productive potential. They are also nine-tenths empty, since the world already has more ships in the 120,000 ton range than it needs. (Eight of them used to be cranked out every year in this one spot.) Engineers of appallingly high rank assembled to assure me that the spare capacity was in the process of being switched to other things. My tour of the factory took in one of the other things – a complete oil refinery about to be floated in its entirety to the Persian Gulf.

In the gear-cutting plant I watched a computerised gantry-mill do its complex number with very few human beings present. Under the Japanese system workers don't get fired, but nobody conceals the fact that more and more of them will have to be retrained as automation steps up. When you add the prospect of zero growth (and even the most optimistic Mitsubishi engineer didn't expect the yards to be operating at capacity again in the next decade) it becomes obvious that jobs must grow fewer.

In Japan the big companies, the *zaibutsu*, are accustomed to controlling events. During the war they even persuaded the Government to compensate them for bomb damage, and the McCarthyite mood of the Occupation ensured that there was no concerted attempt to break up their powerful networks of ownership and administration. A worker in a big company is set for life whatever happens. But not even the big companies can go on expanding when world markets are already saturated; and if they don't expand, there must be a growing number of people who don't get taken on; and the general result must be insecurity. If the Japanese work-force as a whole begins saving its money against a rainy day, who will buy the goods which the Government is encouraging the outside world to send?

The same question reared its lumpy head at my afternoon fixture in Hiroshima, the Toyo Kogyo plant, where they make Mazda rotary-engined cars. Mazda is a middle-sized firm – only about three-quarters of a million units a year –

but the productivity is enough to give a British shop steward heart failure. On the production line I saw four Kawasaki Unimate robot welders zapping *all* the welds on each car body without human assistance or even supervision. The robots were cassette-controlled and could switch programmes automatically according to which model they were working on. Further down the belt, the occasional human being was on hand to hang the boot door. Otherwise it was all machinery, the robots leaning and dabbing like ants milking an aphid.

At Renault and Fiat automation has gone even further, but nobody could be more *efficient* than the Japanese. You can see why it is difficult for a British components manufacturer to supply a Japanese company, even with official encouragement. At Mazda there is hardly any warehouse space for components. Parts for sub-assemblies arrive on the day, even on the hour. Once again the shortage of land dictates the way of doing things.

Rice is a demanding crop. The first thing it demands is a co-operative effort. The whole family has always been involved. Every Japanese company is a direct descendant of the rice culture. All decisions are discussed at every level from the bottom upwards and nobody is allowed to feel unimportant. At Mazda, as at Mitsubishi, the tradition holds. Nobody gets fired, but as the export drive slows down (and at Mazda it is being slowed down voluntarily: their new RX7 sports car would be a sensation here if they released it), they are thinning their work-force by the simple expedient of taking nobody on. The average worker at Mazda is thirty-six years old and has been with the company eleven years. You don't need a pocket calculator to see that the young men who aren't being hired must inevitably swell the number of Japanese citizens who won't be in the market for British exports.

Nevertheless there is no reason for despair, although if there were a single place in Japan calculated to lower your morale, Hiroshima would be it. Even if you think you already know all you need to know about the effects of an atomic bomb, a quick glance around the Memorial Museum still comes as a shock. In the evening I went out with Jun-san and two of his colleagues from JETRO to paint the town. We lined up on the bar-stools of a nightclub called The Bridegroom of the Sea. It was just big enough to hold the four of us. While the lads took turns singing pop songs into a microphone (the bar-girls had endless supplies of back-up tapes, songbooks and fixed grins) I took the only drink I have had in five years and tried to sort out my feelings about Japan's current fix. How can an exporting country with an economy in recession step up its imports? It's like squaring the circle.

Yet in trading with Japan Britain enjoys an advantage that can go a long way towards overcoming even the most ruthless equation. Ever since the Meiji restoration opened them up to Western influence the Japanese have admired the English language and what they conceive to be the British way of life. The Japanese study the English language assiduously and with increasingly less hilarious results. It might raise a smile when Nissan calls a sedan the Cedric; or when the tobacconist offers cigarettes called Hope, Peace, Just, Epsom and Mr Slim; or when you see a bottle of some alcoholic beverage called Fuku Rocks. The older hotels will occasionally regale you with risible warning notices. ('Body posture lower and cover mouth with handkerchief when escape.') The exhibition halls at the Mikimoto Pearl Island feature some choice rubrics about the pearl-diver's career. ('These are man and wife, working in double harness. They sail away into the offing . . . ') But on the whole any funny English you see will date from twenty years ago.

Nowadays the Japanese are so attuned to the English language that they are incorporating it into their own. Through the medium of neon signs, the English alphabet is rapidly being added to the three alphabets that make up Japanese. The tendency to respect any product with an English name is doubled when the name really *is* English, and doubled again when the name is mellowed with age. Burberry, Dunhill and

Hardy Amies are household names in Japan. The connotations are of the Royal family, country life, dogs, grouse.

If I were British Leyland, I would quit trying to sell the Japanese cheap cars and instead penetrate the market at its most vulnerable point – crisps. The Japanese are not yet crisp conscious, but could easily be made so. At present their comparable delicacy is dehydrated octopus shreds, sold in a transparent plastic box. When you open the box the emergent odour throws you for a loop of large radius. I can't believe a Japanese wouldn't rather eat British Leyland crisps. All you would need would be a TV advertising campaign suggesting that British Leyland crisps have been a feature of British life since William the Conqueror and that the Queen is crazy about them.

Considering the effort the Japanese put into learning English, the least a prospective British exporter can do is to make a start on Japanese. The spoken language is not wholly impossible. There is no distinction between singular and plural, for example, which simplifies the grammar. The degrees of politeness are what make the spoken language hard to get the hang of. No one should imagine that he will ever be able to do business in the language, but any attempt at ordinary conversation will be welcomed by the Japanese, who are as hospitable in this respect as the Italians and Russians, and the opposite of the French.

The written language really *is* a challenge. But of the three alphabets, *Katakana* and *Hiragana* are both phonetic and fairly easily learned. Since *Katakana* is used to translate foreign names, half the neon signs in Japan are busy providing you with free look-say language lessons. The name of every railway station appears in *Hiragana* just above an English transcription, so you soon find yourself learning that too. As we travelled on the *Shinkansen*, Jun-san tested me on phonetic alphabets while I gave him exercise on his 'l' sounds. 'You lily-livered lout,' he would recite, 'you left me lying there.' Meanwhile I would shout in triumph at having deciphered a neon sign saying ko-ka ko-ra.

The third alphabet, *Kanji*, is the poser. Composed of roughly 2,000 Chinese ideographs, it is better regarded as a vocabulary than as an alphabet. Japanese children need six years to absorb the first 881 characters, so the beginner can hardly hope to make quick progress. But even then you will find yourself learning a few characters (entrance, exit, up, down, mountain, river, and so on) without really trying. It's a long way from there to the great literary masterpiece *The Tale of Genji* by the Lady Murasaki, but there are more immediate satisfactions. The written language is a pleasure to the eye, thereby conforming to a general cultural pattern in which everyday things are only a step away from art.

From Hiroshima back to Tokyo on the *Shinkansen* is more than five hours of industrial landscape. Millions of compulsive over-achievers were toiling away as I raced past them. Back in Tokyo, I was taken to visit the enormous newspaper *Asahi Shimbun*, whose economics experts lined up on the opposite side of the lunch table to Exchange Views. The picture they drew was slightly different from JETRO's. According to them, the Japanese economy, though it will not collapse before the rest of the world's does, is nevertheless headed for further recession. There will probably be no great political shift: Fukuda might be replaced, but the Liberal Democratic Party will go on ruling, mainly because there is no real Left. (Ripping up Narita airport does not count.) The deciding factor will be if the big companies start to go bankrupt along with the small ones, thereby leading to mass unemployment. Meanwhile there is nothing to do except learn to live with the post-industrial age. The Government can do something to reduce the balance of payments surplus by stockpiling raw materials. But whether it can get the same result by encouraging imports remains problematical. Low domestic demand is unavoidable.

So there it is, and there are even some wise people who are glad. The most impressive man I met in Japan, Kazayuki Matsuo, of the American History department at Tokyo's Sophia University, thinks that economic success has produced a kind of Hell, that the Bullet Train simply takes people nowhere at a greater rate, and that what Japan needs is more of the English disease. Japanese domestic life, he believes, has become a disaster, in which tired husbands stagger home late to wives who have nothing to live for except television and *pachinko*, a mindless version of pinball.

I could see his point, but was still glad that however Japan's future is settled, it will probably not be by war. Looking south-west from the top of a skyscraper on my last day in Tokyo, I could see all the way to Fuji – about 150 miles. The whole stretch of coast was full of people, and beyond the holy mountain they went on and on. The first B-29s appeared over Japanese mainland targets on the night of June 14, 1944. They spent more than a year bombing Japan out of the war. The big cities burned well. The official USAF figure for the great Tokyo fire-raid was 86,000 dead, and the Japanese put it at more than twice that.

The cumulative effect of the fire-raids and the atomic bombs was to convince Japan that she was forever out of the running as a military super-power. Remembering too well what happened last time, the Japanese now have no thought of overcoming trade restrictions by any other means than brains and skill. Another war in the Pacific has become unthinkable. In Australia I grew up with the constant reminder that a generation of our best men had been decimated. One of the victims was my father, who was a POW in Japanese hands. His sufferings were so terrible that perhaps it was a blessing he did not come home, but thirty years later I still feel that my whole life is taking place in the light of that one event. I had expected to be depressed by the Japanese. In fact I was exhilarated, because in a way they are showing us that the future is still worth looking forward to.

One day all the world will be like Japan, full of more and more people with less and less to do. We can scarcely hope to make the transition better than Japan is doing. To a remarkable extent she has preserved the old along with the new, and preserved her own culture while absorbing an extraordinary amount of everybody else's. In Japan you can see how the collective and the individual spirits need not necessarily crush one another.

By now a dab hand with the chopsticks, I dined out on my last night with Jun-san the PR-man and the boys from JETRO. Saying goodbye is always a lengthy process in Japan. I was sorry to be going, but by now I was burning to be alone. After twelve days of propinquity, what the Westerner needs is unpeopled space. JAL provided some. Refuelling at Anchorage, Alaska, my Boeing 747 made a beeline for Copenhagen. It was a relief to look down on the North Pole. Not even the Japanese could do much with that.

June 11, 1978

Postcard from Biarritz

THE WEEKLY Air France Caravelle to Biarritz took off from Heathrow only an hour late. The French air-traffic controllers must have slipped up. Most other flights routed over French air-space were being delayed for days on end, with passengers eating one another in the airports. But by some miracle we had been allowed through.

Nor were we intercepted en route. I was fully expecting a squadron of Mirage jet fighters to come screaming out of the sun and shoot us down. Not a bit of it. Popping the odd rivet, our ageing but trusty Caravelle made a gallant left turn over the Coast of Silver and alighted with its characteristic hot landing speed – none of that reverse thrust nonsense, just turn off the power and wait until she stops rolling – on the mini-golf course that Biarritz calls an airport.

Biarritz receives you like a clapped-out Disneyland with brains. In the days when the place was an amusement park for the rich, they outdid one another building holiday homes that would express their high spirits. The high spirits were mainly induced by the fact that they were not obliged to share the bracing ozone with the lower orders. Nowadays anybody is allowed in. When anybody arrives, he finds the enchanted playground looking pretty much as its upper-crust habitués left it. He also finds the ozone as bracing as it ever was, the beaches just as long, the water just as warm, the sunsets just as gorgeous, and the young ladies wearing far fewer clothes. The great days of Biarritz are over, but the nice days might just be beginning.

This was my second visit to Biarritz. Last year at about the same date I went down there to work on a film script with my compatriot, the theatre director Michael Blakemore, who owns a house on the Rue Gambetta, right in the middle of town. Most of Biarritz is in the middle of town. The beaches are endless, with real sand on them, but the town itself is quite small. Turning some of his iffy West End earnings into a tangible asset, Blakemore bought the house seven years ago. The purchase cleaned him out, but the climate, cliffs and waves reminded him of home. They did the same to me. We spent two weeks not writing a film. This year we planned to spend another two weeks not writing a play.

Biarritz is on the Atlantic coast of France, just north of the Spanish border, which puts it in the Basque country. It used to be a fishing village before it became the most fashionable resort of the nineteenth century. With the end of the *belle époque* it went into a long decline, until by now the place is so far out that it's almost on its way back in. People are starting to recognise the name again, even if they can't say exactly where it is, or even tell the Côte d'Argent from the Côte d'Azur. Biarritz is starting to revive. But there are ways in which the prospect of renewed vitality is a pity as well as a blessing.

In the twelfth century the Basque fishermen of Biarritz used to hunt whales with deadly efficiency. When the whales sensibly moved away, the Basques chased them further and further, with the consequence that the fishermen of Biarritz discovered America before Columbus did. (This is a matter for local pride but on a larger view it is not quite so stunning, since with the possible exception of the Swiss everybody discovered America before Columbus did.)

Having too small a port for deep-sea trading, Biarritz became a backwater and stayed that way until a certain Spanish noblewoman started sending her daughter there for the annual holidays. The daughter married Napoleon III of France, became the Empress Eugénie, and persuaded her husband that Biarritz was the ideal place for the Second Empire to set up its summer headquarters. Together, in the late 1850s, they built the Résidence Eugénie. Biarritz rapidly became the Beach of the Kings – a title it kept in good repair until the last spasm of the *belle époque*.

They all turned up. Reigning monarchs from all over Europe headed for Biarritz in special trains. Deposed monarchs went into exile there. Maharajas moved in. There was a commingling of crowns, a tangling of tiaras. Even after the Empire fell, the season didn't slow down for a minute. In fact it lasted the whole year round. The English, a hardy breed, were there all winter. The Russians were there in the autumn, the French and Spanish in the spring and summer. The Empress Elizabeth of Austria was a regular. So, eventually, was the Prince of Wales, who acquired much of his girth in the Biarritz pastry shops and as Edward VII continued to favour the town with his massive presence, thereby laying the foundations of its lasting fondness for the English.

Why did the princes of the blood and all their parasites like Biarritz so much and for so long? Part of the answer was that it cost so much to get there. The train fare from Paris to the Normandy beaches was only 25 francs. From Paris to Biarritz was 125. So the commonalty couldn't afford to make the trip. That left the nobs free to hob with one another. The word democracy was probably never mentioned except in jest.

Yet paradoxically the nobility and the high bourgeoisie gave more to Biarritz than they ever took away. Private patronage resulted in an astonishing array of public works. On Eugénie's orders, a tunnel was driven through the rocks to give access from the Grande Plage in the north to the Côte des Basques in the south. Miles of walkways appeared, all lined with tamarisks and hydrangeas. Casinos and grand hotels duly materialised. Everyone who was anyone built a château or a villa. Architecture was encouraged to reflect the festive mood by running riot. Turrets, gables, gazebos and similar ridiculosities proliferated, forming a pop-up picture-book skyline against the pink extravaganza of the sunset.

Mad with enthusiasm, some of the more adventurous spirits even dared to immerse themselves in the sea. Previously the idea had not occurred to anyone. Eugénie had not been the only illustrious name to admire the onrushing ocean of Biarritz and environs. Stendhal, Taine, Flaubert, Victor Hugo and other great romantics had all, at one time or another, pronounced themselves awed by the remorseless waves. But it was a long step from admiring them to actually getting in amongst them. Eventually the fad caught on, but like every other nineteenth-century diversion it was accompanied by a lot of ritualised fuss and elaborate machinery.

Even in the closing years of the *belle époque*, a fashionable lady in full walking-out regalia needed a moving staircase, or *trottoir roulant*, to get her and her various attendants down to the beach. Once there, she disappeared into *la cabine de l'établissement* and spent three-quarters of an hour getting changed for an encounter with the waters that was never allowed to exceed more than a few minutes, lest death intervene.

Having approached the water's edge, she was divested of her *peignoir* by a *guide-baigneur* and stood provokingly revealed – still fully dressed from neck to knee, but marginally less voluminously. The *guides-baigneurs*, most of them Basques, were themselves fully dressed, including straw hat: only their hands, feet and that part of the face not covered by a handle-bar moustache could be regarded as bare.

While one *guide-baigneur* alertly held the *peignoir*, another *guide-baigneur*, or in the case of more exalted clients two other *guides-baigneurs*, accompanied the lady a few inches into the pitiless torrent. Supported by her muscular champions, the lady gave herself up to the mercy of the deep. What went on beneath the waves must remain forever unknown, but one trusts that class barriers were suitably eroded. Ankles must have touched. Knees must have collided. Surely the occasional rendezvous was made, as it is today in the winter resorts, where fine ladies sometimes invite their ski instructors to bed, although never to dinner.

Upon her retreat from the pounding *vagues*, the lady was once again enveloped in her *peignoir* and escorted back up the beach for another three-quarters of an hour in *la cabine*, after which the *trottoir roulant* was ready to hoist her back to civilisation. The rest of the day could be spent discussing her adventure with other ladies of her own rank.

The whole routine went without a hitch until the day in 1908 when the Comtesse de Madron put her foot in it. She got one of her buttoned boots caught in the mechanism of the *trottoir roulant*. Minus four toes, she sued everyone, and the offending device, like so much else, was closed down for keeps in 1914.

Sealed in a bubble of indifference, Biarritz was preserved by neglect. Two World Wars with a Depression in between left it looking pretty much as it had been when life was still sweet. Art deco was added to the conglomerate of styles; another Prince of Wales, thinner this time, was added to the aggregate of princely visitors; but the old confidence was gone. The fashionable action moved to the Mediterranean. Biarritz still served the turn as a plush funk-hole, but as a display case it was past tense. The postcards on sale from year to year showed little that was altered, still less that was new. During the Second World War the Germans installed concrete gun emplacements to enfilade the beaches in case the Allies tried a right hook. The Allies never came and the gun emplacements, too solid to blow up, were turned into flower-beds.

To put it cruelly, Biarritz became a ghost town – a magnificent but dispirited relic of the old Europe. After the Second World War the high-born and well-placed still came for the season, but only if they were of a certain age. Their sons and daughters went to St Tropez, where the waves were very flat but there was a chance of seeing Brigitte Bardot's behind. Nobody thought of the big waves at Biarritz with any special fondness until 1956, when Richard Zanuck and Peter Viertel arrived on the coast to scout locations for *The Sun Also Rises*.

Zanuck was the producer of the movie and Viertel was the writer. The minute they clapped eyes on the surf at Biarritz they started not producing and not writing. They had their surfboards shipped over from California. These were Malibu, or hot-dog, surfboards, the ancestors of the potato-chip surfboards in use today. When Zanuck and Viertel stood up on the waves, the locals were variously outraged and enchanted. Some of the village elders said it was against the laws of both God and gravity. But the younger men couldn't wait to join in.

Few Frenchmen had ever gone in for body-surfing, and you still don't see much of it even now. As a direct result of the long season Zanuck and Viertel spent not working on *The Sun Also Rises*, the French think of surfing as an activity carried out exclusively on surfboards. Old Australian crocks like Blakemore and myself can occasionally be seen shooting the breakers on our bare chests – all right, bare stomachs – but for the natives surfing is something you do standing up.

The awful truth is that young people all over the world think the same way. My generation has been bypassed. On the Sydney beaches when I was young, a surfboard was something only a weightlifter could ride: built of wood, it went straight for the beach like a landing barge while the rider crouching on top of it pretended to be in control. The first Malibu boards arrived at about the time I left, so I never learned to ride one. In fact I never even touched one until I met Peter Viertel in Biarritz. Viertel has white hair by now but his way of life – which includes being married to Deborah Kerr – keeps him young. He can still stand on the waves like a boy on a dolphin. Under his tuition I finally got to stand up on a surfboard, if only for a few seconds. It feels great.

Surfing has helped to revive the energies of Biarritz. Surfers come there from all over Europe and indeed the world: a new, penniless royalty. There are elegant French surfers with degrees in science, stunning wives or husbands, and surfboards with sails on them. There are German surfers who look as if they took up the sport because terrorism was too much like work. You see van-loads of Australians with John Newcombe moustaches and countersunk eyes like tacks in a carpet. Half my age and not even sure which country they are in, the Australians climb into their Rip Curl wet-suits and sit for hours half a mile off the Côte des Basques, patiently waiting for a wave worthy of their steel. Last year, on a flat day, I heard one of them say: 'Shit, this is no good. Let's go to Spain.'

Usually it is good enough. You can see why a generation brought up on skateboards, surfboards and *Crystal Voyager* should want to make Biarritz one of their summer stopovers. Unfortunately, from the viewpoint of the municipality, the surfing boom is not enough by itself to generate prosperity. Too many surfers are bums. They sleep in a van, dry their clothes on top of it, eat off the pavement and don't even tip the lady in the WC. Most of the cash is brought to town by ordinary people who wouldn't mind if the surf disappeared tomorrow, so long as the sand was still there.

Wealth resides not in the few hundred surfers but in the thousands of ordinary paddlers who bring their children. As the old hotels continue to rot away, it looks like common sense to replace them with the kind of modern building that will pack the punters in more efficiently. Alas, the results are horrible to behold. Rearing up out of Biarritz's otherwise dinky eclecticism, the typical new hotels look like a cross between a typewriter and a toilet. So far there are only about a dozen of them, but they point the way that things might go. By now the original buildings are falling down of their own accord. To restore and maintain so many bizarre old edifices would seem quixotic even supposing it were technically possible. The temptation to let them all collapse is reinforced by the suspicion that most holidaymakers wouldn't care. What they want is hot showers that work. Yet a compromise ought to be possible. Perhaps the interiors could be gutted and the façades kept – apart from people in the social swim, nobody ever saw what was behind them anyway.

Biarritz is a jumble of a town and no single solution to its problems can possibly be right. The Basques being a fiery lot, they might easily talk themselves into a ruinous snap decision concerning the town's most immediate problem, which is what to do about the advancing sea. On the Côte des Basques the beach is reputedly getting smaller year by year, while the cliffs show a disconcerting tendency to cave in, with detrimental effects on property values. The mayor is in favour of a scheme by which piers would be built at regular intervals, thereby producing a string of bijou beachettes with plenty of sand in them but no surf. This is a notch better than an earlier scheme to turn the whole beach into a marina, but it still ranks as a catastrophe, since even the non-surfing Basque elders are well aware that the unbroken line of *sable d'or* on the Côte des Basques is the chief glory of Biarritz.

I went to a public meeting at which the mayor proposed his scheme at enormous length. A spoke was put in his wheel by a prodigiously ancient Basque who got to his feet – this process in itself consuming a good proportion of the evening – and announced that the Côte des Basques was exactly the same now as it had been when he was a boy. The meeting erupted. People were screaming at one another. Suddenly it was easy to see why successive Spanish Governments, whether of the Left or the Right, have always found it hard to keep the Basques in line.

If you drive down to San Sebastian the Spanish Basques will serve you a dish of prawns cooked in salt that taste better than anything else you have ever eaten. Unfortunately they might also blow up your car. The Basques are simply an explosive people. They play half a dozen different versions of *pelote*. One version is played with the bare hand, which comes to resemble a catcher's mitt. The fastest version, *cesta punta*, is played with a long basket strapped to the right wrist. The venue is a sort of giant squash court and the ball travels fast enough to kill. The players wear crash helmets and spend a lot of time falling on their heads.

The chummiest version of *pelote* is called *grande chistera*. It is played with the long basket but in the open air and against only one wall. The game is not quite as sensational as *cesta punta* but it involves the spectators in a big way, since there is no net between them and the action. If you take your eyes off the ball you can end up with a bad headache. A girl sitting only a few feet away from me got absorbed in conversation with her boyfriend. They had only just arrived. He was watching the ball and she wasn't. It hit her in the right temple. He had to take her home. Having just blown 30 francs in a matter of seconds, he was one very embittered Basque.

The Basques were in Biarritz before the whales went away and will probably be there when they come back. But in the mean time they are willing to make the rest of us feel welcome. There has probably never been a better time in Biarritz than now. The old days had a lot of style but little substance. Think of all those elegantly turned-out gentlemen lined up on the esplanade and searching the beach for the glimpse of an ankle. Nowadays you can see some of the most heartbreakingly pretty girls in the world springing around with hardly anything on at all. Sucking in our paunches, Blakemore and I stride seawards in a masterful manner. Can anyone doubt that life today is better, now that the gap between those who lie about and those who work for a living has narrowed to the point that they are often the same people? Anyway, as a place in which not to do something, Biarritz is unbeatable. Already we have not written a film and a play. Next year we might not write a musical.

August 27, 1978

Postcard from Rome

B RITISH Airways were justifiably proud of getting your correspondent to Rome only three hours behind schedule. After all, Heathrow had been in the grip of those freak snow conditions which traditionally leave Britain stunned with surprise.

In England, British Rail loudspeakers had been smugly announcing prolonged delays due to locomotives coming into contact with inexplicable meteorological phenomena, such as heaps of water lying around in frozen form. Airport officials were equally flabbergasted to discover more of the same stuff falling out of the sky. But now my staunch Trident was leaving all that behind. In a dark but clear midnight, Rome lay below. Those strings of lights were roads all leading to the same place.

All my previous visits to the Eternal City had been done on the cheap. In those days I was still travelling on the weird escape routes frequented by students. Some of the students turned out to be eighty-year-old Calabrian peasant ladies carrying string bags full of onions. The charter aircraft belonged to semi-scheduled airlines whose pilots wore black

73

eyepatches and First World War medals. Their point of arrival was Ciampino, Rome's no. 2 airport – an inglorious military establishment ringed with flat-tyred DC-4s and Convair 240s too obsolete for anything except fire drill.

I used to live in the kind of cold-water *pensione* on the Via del Corso where the original rooms had been partitioned not only vertically but horizontally as well, so that the spiral staircase beside your bed led up to a bare ceiling. You had to apply in writing to take a bath. Lunch was half a plate of pasta on the other side of the Tiber. Dinner was the other half.

A lot of water has gone over the viaduct since then, and this time I was a *bona fide* traveller. Even at one o'clock in the morning Leonardo da Vinci airport, tastefully done out in fluted chromium, was a treat for the eyes. My hotel was in Piazza Trinità dei Monti at the very top of the Spanish Steps. The décor was strictly veneers and cut glass, but it was heavily tricked out with the Medici coat of arms and the bath came ready equipped not just with a plug, but a dinky sachet of foam-producing green goo. My waiting readers were subsidising this luxury. Could I justify their confidence? What can you say about so old a city in so short a space? I sank cravenly into the foam.

Sleep allayed my fears, but they came back in the morning. I appeared on the Spanish Steps just in time to be greeted by the cold weather, which had been racing down Europe during the night. Rome suddenly froze up solid. The Triton, forever blowing his conch in the Piazza Barberini, abruptly became festooned with icicles. As unashamedly ostentatious as ever, the wealthier Roman women shopping in the Via Condotti instantly adopted a uniform – mink and boots. In a bar a little fat lady who looked like a bale of furs reached up to spoon the cream from a glass of hot chocolate higher than her head. For once nobody was in any danger of being kidnapped. Cold weather meant plenty of snow in the mountain resorts. The terrorists were all away skiing.

With only a few days at my disposal I decided to leave

most of my usual haunts unvisited, apart from a quick trip to St Peter's to see how well the Michelangelo *pietà* had been repaired. Since I had last seen this masterpiece it had been attacked by a hammer-wielding Australian of Hungarian origins. Perhaps he was trying to effect improvements. Anyway, he had given the Madonna a nose-job. The nose was now back on and the whole statue, I was glad to see, had been separated from its adoring public by a glass wall. Taking it for granted that none of my compatriots had been flicking ink darts at the Sistine ceiling, I headed out by car to the Catacombs.

Out on the old Appian Way it was as cold as Caligula's heart. Sleet drenched the roadside ruins. Like a leftover from *La Strada*, a lone whore solicited business from passing cars. A couple of millennia ago the cars would have been chariots but she would have looked roughly the same. Hilarius Fuscus has a tomb out there somewhere. Apart from his name he is of no historical interest, but with a name like Hilarius Fuscus how interesting do you have to be? The Catacombs, however, were mainly for the nameless. In the Catacombs of Domitilla, for example, more than 100,000 people were buried, but only seventy of them came down to modern times with any identity beyond that conferred by the heap of powder their bones turned into when touched by air.

A German monk took me down into the ground. 'Zer soil is called tufa. Volcanig. Easy for tunnels. Mind zer head.' In this one set of catacombs there are eleven miles of tunnels, one network under another. The two top levels have electric light throughout. 'Mine apologies for zer electric light. Mit candles is more eery. Zis way.' People had been filed away down here by the generation. Some of the frescos remain intelligible. You can see the style changing through time: suddenly a Byzantine Christ tells you that the Empire of the West is in decline. The sign of the fish is everywhere. 'You also see zer sign of zer turdle dove. Symbol of luff und piss.'

When we arrived back at the surface the good friar's next party was alighting from its coach – a couple of hundred

Japanese, all of them with cameras round their necks. Some of the cameras had tripods attached. I had been lucky to get what amounted to a private view. Nor were there many tourists at the newest of the Catacombs, the Fosse Ardeatine. The people buried here all died at once, on March 24, 1944. For the whole story you have to go to Anzio, about thirty-five miles down the coast.

Anzio is a small town built around a port. A few hundred yards from the port there are some ruined foundations on a low cliff. Standing in the ruins, you can look along the beaches. The Allied forces came ashore here in January 1944. The landing was unopposed but it took a long time to develop a beach-head. Italy was already out of the war but the Germans were not: far from it. Kesselring counterattacked with horrific violence. The whole area became an enormous battlefield. The flat littoral terrain was ideal for the German armour. Right over your head, the Ju88s came bombing and strafing. The Allied forces were stymied for months.

In Rome, the Italian resistance fighters grew tired of waiting. They ambushed an SS detachment in the Via Rasella, just down from the gates of the Palazzo Barberini, killing thirty-two men. Hitler ordered reprisals at the rate of ten to one. The SS, enthusiastically exceeding requirements, trucked 335 people out to the Fosse Ardeatine and shot them all.

But back to those ruins at Anzio. I am still standing in them, a bedraggled figure washed by the rain. They are the ruins of Nero's seaside villa. And back in time beyond Nero, on that low hill behind the town, Cicero had the country house of whose amenities he boasted in his letters to Atticus. In those days Anzio was called Antium. Further back than that, Coriolanus went into exile here. And even further back, at about the time the city of Rome was being founded – the year zero *ab urbe condita* – Antium was one of the main hangouts of the dreaded Volsci.

The Volsci feature on almost every page in the early books of Livy. The Romans were still confined to an area about the size of Hampstead and whenever they ventured outside their seven hills they had the Volsci breathing garlic down their necks. Eventually, through discipline, the Romans prevailed. That was Livy's message to his contemporary readers: remember your origins.

Everything and everywhere in and around Rome is saturated with time. If you look too long, you will be hypnotised. I went out to Lago Albano in the Alban Hills. The lake is in a giant crater. High on the rim is a town called Marino, where Sophia Loren owns a house. The Pope's summer residence is somewhere up there too. But take a close look at that sheltered lake. Imagine it in tumult. In Imperial times it was called Lacus Albanus and mock naval battles were held on it. That would have been my job in those days: writing reviews of mock naval battles. 'Once again Hilarius Fuscus made mincemeat of the opposition . . . '

Until recently, Sophia Loren faced serious charges with regard to the national currency. She was accused of trying to export some of her money. Almost everybody who owns any has been doing the same, but Sophia is supposed to be a woman of the people. Even the Press has turned against her. Her latest film has been greeted with massed raspberries. I went to see it. The critics were right.

The movie is directed by Lina Wertmueller and is crisply entitled *Fatto di sangue tra due uomini per causa di una vedova: si sospettano moventi politici*. This may be loosely rendered as 'A matter of honour between two men because of a widow: political motives are suspected.' My translation loses something of the original's flaccidity. Ms Wertmueller has an international reputation but her idea of a joke reveals her to be a humourless scold. The movie is all about hard times in Sicily. Apart from Sophia, it is a disaster. Sophia, playing a passionate charcoal-burner, looks better than ever and acts a storm. It is ridiculous that so life-giving an individual should be made a scapegoat.

The same thought occurred to me when I attended a Rome Opera production of Bellini's *I Capuletti ed i Montecchi*. Romeo and Juliet both sang magnificently. The settings were a reminder of how a lot can be made out of little – Covent Garden please copy. The audience in the stalls consisted mainly of the Roman bourgeoisie. They behaved like pigs. A man near me recited the whole plot to his deaf wife while she ate chocolate which had apparently been wrapped in dead leaves. The stalls were empty before the curtain calls were half over. But the gallery went crazy with gratitude.

Here was an opera company for any city to be proud of. Yet half of its members are in trouble with the police because of alleged corruption. While terrorists maim and murder at will, the cops are chasing contraltos. It's a clear case of fiddling while Rome burns.

In the Via Michelangelo Caetani a shrine of wreaths and photographs marks the spot where ex-Prime Minister Moro's body was dumped midway between the respective headquarters of the Communists and the Christian Democrats. To the terrorists, Moro stood for compromise. It followed logically that his life was forfeit. Most of the terrorists are *figli di papà* – sons of daddy. If daddy spends most of his time making money, shooting him is a good way of getting his attention. Under the absolutism there is petulance.

There have been bodies in that street before. As the Middle Ages gave way to the Renaissance, the Caetani fought the Colonna who fought the Orsini who fought the Caetani. Rienzo called himself tribune and reunited Rome for a few days. The great families used the Papacy to further their earthly ambitions. But ever since the fall of the old Empire the very idea of a renewed temporal hegemony had been an empty dream.

As Machiavelli bitterly noted, the Church, while not powerful enough to unite the country, was certainly powerful enough to make sure nobody else did. Machiavelli's remarks on the topic remain pertinent today, when even the Christian Democrats are appalled at the prospect of a Pope who seems intent on discrediting the legislature over the matter of abortion. The last thing the country needs is any more dividing. Italy's besetting weakness is government without authority. The result is not sweet anarchy but gun law.

You don't have to go all the way out to the Alban Hills in order to look down on Rome and discover it to be a small place. All you have to do is climb the Aventine. What you can see from there is just about all there is. When Rome ceased to be the capital city of an international empire, it reverted to being a provincial town. Though it has been officially called so since 1870, it has never really become the capital of Italy – not in the way London is the capital of England or Paris of France. Rome produces little. For a long time it has been a consumers' town. Even the Renaissance was produced in Florence and consumed in Rome. Bringing Michelangelo to Rome was like bringing Tolstoy to Hollywood.

Rome is a good place for madmen to dream of building empires. It is a bad place from which to govern Italy. Mussolini chose the first option, with the inevitable consequences. The most recent of Rome's overlords, he left the fewest traces. Apart from the embarrassingly fine architecture of the EUR district out on the periphery, the city gives almost no indication that he ever lived. The Palazzo di Venezia is, of course, still there. You can pick out the balcony from which he shouted to the crowds and the window behind which he left a light burning at night to encourage the notion that he never slept. Wealthy ladies used to visit him there, but by all accounts his technique as a lover was long on preliminary chest-beating and short on follow-through. It seems that he just hurled them to the floor and passed over them in a shallow dive.

The reason that the Empire could never be restored was that the world grew out of it. The Roman Empire died of success. It was already dying when Scipio Africanus became the first Roman to take a bath as often as once a week. It was already dying when the legions in Sicily met their first Greeks and began learning the ways of cultivated leisure. Livy's history is one long lament for the old Republic – a warning to

Augustus that the tribe's disciplined impulse was on the wane.

But Livy never saw that he himself was part of the problem. Nor did Tacitus at a later time. The city which had once been little more than a base camp had become a civilisation. It was changing at the centre. The decline was really a transformation. The Empire became the Church, which became other churches, which became the Enlightenment, which became the modern age. The centurions became the priests who became us. With the eyes history has given us, we can now see that to unite the world is no longer a sane aim. It has already become united, within the individual soul.

Meanwhile the city of Rome is left with nothing but its heritage. There is a lot to look after. Things get stolen, or just fall apart. In the Piazza Navona I found the Bernini fountains plump with ice, like overfilled tubs of lemon *gelato*. In a dark alley behind the piazza stands the little church of Santa Maria della Pace. On the outside walls are the usual political graffiti. Inside there are some sibyls by Raphael. The doors are open only between 7 and 8.30 in the morning, for Mass. Outside the portico when I arrived, the body of a man was being hauled out of an abandoned car and loaded into a grey plastic bag. He was a tramp who had frozen to death in the night. A policeman signed for the corpse. Dirt, litter and decay. Raffaello Sanzio of Urbino was here once.

But it's unfair on Rome to let the weather get you down. In spring and summer the fountains ionise the air to the point that even the third-rate expatriate American writers who infest the city feel themselves brimming over with creative energy. Yet even then you can detect the weariness beneath the fervour. No less afraid of dying than anybody else, I still like the idea of what Lucretius describes as the reef of destruction to which all things must tend, *spatio aetatis defessa vetusto* – worn out by the ancient lapse of years. But I don't want to see the reef every day.

The Spanish Steps were a cataract. Climbing them like an exhausted salmon, I passed the window of the room in which

Keats coughed out the last hours of his short life with nothing to look at except a cemetery of time. No wonder he forgot his own vitality and declared that his name was writ in water. As he should have realised, the thing to do when you feel like that is to pack up and catch a plane to London. Which I did.

February 11, 1979

Postcard from Los Angeles

1 No Stopping Any Time

SURFING in the jet stream created by the polar wind as it curved down across the Atlantic, my Pan Am Boeing 747 made landfall somewhere over Newfoundland, crossed into the United States over Minnesota and found clear air above the snowfields of Colorado. A storm took back the half-hour we had gained. We landed at Los Angeles just ahead of the rain.

I didn't really want to get off. The in-flight movie had been *California Suite*, in which there is a scene where Maggie Smith, playing an English actress flying to Los Angeles for the Academy Award ceremonies in which she will find out whether she has won the Oscar for Best Supporting Actress, watches an in-flight movie about herself flying in an aircraft through a raging storm. For this very role, the real-life Maggie Smith had just been nominated for Best Supporting Actress. Flying along with earphones plugged into my head while watching Maggie Smith flying along with earphones

81

plugged into her head watching herself flying along, I had suffered a partial collapse of the will to live. The twentieth century was getting too complicated for a simple soul to cope with.

When I finally staggered off the plane and claimed my luggage, it seemed only natural that Bruce Forsyth should come running towards me in the reception area. I couldn't remember what I had written about him that had been so bad, but in these days of instant travel there was no reason why he should not have chosen LA airport as the site of my execution. I shut my eyes and waited for the blow. When I opened them again, it was to discover that he had run past me and was embracing somebody else.

Los Angeles had been coming to me all my life, but this was the first time I had come to it. Prejudices are useless. Call Los Angeles any dirty name you like – Six Suburbs in Search of a City, Paradise with a Lobotomy, anything – but the fact remains that you are already living in it before you get there.

The city's layout is a tangle of circumferences which have lost contact with their centres. It all makes sense as long as you can drive. Unfortunately I can't. Or rather I can, but nobody believes in my ability enough to give me a licence. So instead of hiring a car I had to head for my motel by cab. On the San Diego freeway it was like stock-car racing. Pick-ups with flambeau paint-jobs, fat back tyres and bulges on their bonnets went past on either side like bullets, nose down with a gear to spare. Painted like one of Altdorfer's blue night skies fretted with flames, a customised van overtook us, paused long enough for us to absorb the fact that we were looking at the back end of the MIKE VANCE CREATIVE THINKING CENTER MOBILE PLANNING UNIT, and then zoomed away. Despite the comparatively low speed-limit, nobody seemed capable of going slowly. A minatory billboard loomed. 'I TRIED FOUR MORTUARIES – FOREST LAWN WAS LOWER.' MRS JACKIE MULLINS.

My motel, which I shall call the Casa Nervosa because I wouldn't want you to come crashing in and spoil its exclusive atmosphere, lay on Santa Monica Boulevard, near where it bends towards Hollywood. Somebody had tried to make contact with the previous occupant of my room by kicking in the door. There was a swimming pool which by some fluke did not contain a floating body. This was the very motel in which Andy Warhol had filmed one of his nerveless epics. Not even the rain could completely eliminate the lingering aroma of Joe Dallesandro's hair oil. As the sudden night fell, I waited alertly for the scream of Robert having his nipple pierced.

But there was no time to waste. Barely pausing to change, shave and order another cab on a telephone still hot from Sylvia Miles's breath, I raced to Outpost Drive in Hollywood. Here I was to attend the small buffet supper marking the opening night of Gore Vidal's newly decorated house. The concrete footpath was still drying when I arrived. Hysterical with jet-lag, I narrowly avoided falling into it and thus becoming the first total nonentity to have his entire body immortalised in Hollywood cement.

Ushered politely in, I leant weakly against the wall while vainly searching the magnificent interior for an unfamiliar face. Joanne Woodward, Paul Newman, James Coburn, Stefanie Powers, Anthony Perkins, Mia Farrow, Jean-Pierre Aumont and William Holden were all present. I was introduced to Paul Newman. Well, how else do you expect me to say it? That I was introduced to Paul Klutz? Newman looked at me with eyes like chips of frozen sky. He was fascinated. It had probably been twenty years since a face he didn't recognise had got close enough to him for him to realise that he didn't recognise it.

Desperately I hunted for someone obscure enough to talk to. There was nobody. Finally I settled for George Segal. Momentarily diverted by the novel experience of conversing with somebody he had never heard of, Segal listened amiably while I told him how the film on the plane had been about Maggie Smith watching a film on a plane and in this film on the plane she was watching a film about herself on another plane. Segal looked very interested, as if he were

83

rediscovering something. Success had cut him off from this kind of boredom. Stardom can be limiting.

Next morning I was bowling along the freeway under a clear sky in a 1964 drop-head Cadillac chauffeured by Hector and Alphonse, two young men who until the day before had been working as carpenters in Vidal's house but had now decided to start a new career as assistant journalists. Brilliantly overqualified for the task – Hector was a botany student and Alphonse a marine architect – they knew everything about LA.

The city had long ago come alive for me in Rayner Banham's classic book *Los Angeles*, but not even Banham's electrifying writing can give you a full idea of the sheer size of the place. Around the original Spanish settlement, the Pueblo of Our Lady Queen of the Angels, has grown up a city seventy miles square. You can stay on the freeway all day without retracing your tracks by even a yard, and not for a minute will you ever leave Los Angeles.

Over a period of less than a hundred years the city has been happening like a volcanic eruption that solidifies into people and places, but never quite stops moving. Los Angeles has an economy bigger than India's. If California were to secede from the Union it would be the world's sixth richest country. None of these statistics seems at all surprising when the inexhaustible productivity of the place is flowing past your shoulder.

The sources of wealth are all in amongst each other, as if the buried cities of Troy were all on the one level and still functioning. The oilfields are in amongst the original citrus groves. The dockyards are in amongst the oilfields. Within the city limits, there are as many airports as film studios. Aerospace and electronics industries that set world standards share security fences with service industries that launder roller towels. Restaurants look like car washes, car washes look like art galleries, art galleries look like war memorials, war memorials look like fire stations, fire stations look like churches, churches look like restaurants. Everybody has an idea to sell. BALL PARK FRANKS SWELL UP WHEN COOKED. Some ideas look doomed to fail. DAVE'S ACCORDION SCHOOL.

Except for Simon Rodia's famous towers, Watts is a sad sight. Watts isn't even a ghetto. It's nothing. The inhabitants of Chinatown, Little Mexico and Little Japan at least know where they live. But Watts is Little Nowhere. Yet even here the poverty is relative. Waiting around for some trouble to get into, the young blacks are sitting in cars only a few years out of date. There is land around the houses, and although all the walls are thick with aerosol graffiti the sidewalks are not much less clean than anywhere else in LA – which means, by British standards, that they are spotless.

The anti-littering law is backed up by a $500 fine and a famously gung-ho police force equipped like an army. The LA cops will body-search anybody whose name is already in one of their computers. If you try to double-park in downtown LA they will cone you with search-lights, drop on you out of the sky and stick their finger up your behind.

A few miles south of Watts and you are in amongst the biggest, richest port in the world. The oil pumps march straight through the harbour and out to sea. Oil refineries butt against one another like games of draughts that have only just begun. The docks are so enormous that at first the *Queen Mary* looks like a miniature of herself, but no, she really is the *Queen Mary*.

Before you drive north along the beaches, you have to circumvent Palos Verdes on a climbing, dipping and winding road. This is rattlesnake country. Now the Pacific horizon is high beside you on the left. Suddenly you are in the Slide Area. NO STOPPING ANY TIME. At Portuguese Bend the road is like a Moebius strip made of toffee, daily getting further lost in its own contortions. Palos Verdes is still climbing out of the sea. Disaster movies like *Earthquake* are made from the heart. The whole of Los Angeles is built on top of a severe case of geological dyspepsia.

From Palos Verdes you descend to the beaches. Really

they are all the one beach, the Beach, running north in an unbroken sequence from here to Malibu. This is Beach Boy country, where the only challenges are to find the perfect wave and to stay slim. Onwards through King Harbour, Hermosa, El Segundo and Marina del Rey the signs unceasingly dare you to see how much you can consume and still float. BEACHBUM BURT'S CASUAL CUISINE (SUNDAY CHAMPAGNE BRUNCH). The season has barely begun but already the girls look good enough to eat. Despite its billing, so does the food. INCREDIBLE EDIBLES.

Santa Monica was the first stretch of beach the Angelenos ever colonised. Now it is a city of its own. This is custom-car headquarters of the universe. Bodyshops abound. Every kind of car ever made in the world can be seen in its original form on the streets of Los Angeles. Where the original has been lost, a 'replicar' replaces it. But in Santa Monica strange, twisted cars the world has never seen before are born out of troubled dreams. It must be the food. DEL TACO DRIVE-THRU HAMBURGERS.

Beyond Santa Monica the Beach starts curving left at Pacific Palisades. By the time it gets to Malibu it is no longer for the general public, since the beach houses of the wealthy shut it off from easy access. But Pacific Palisades is also the place where Sunset Boulevard starts its long run inland. Now you are in amongst the hills and canyons where those who have really made it have their principal houses. In Bel Air and Beverly Hills those houses which are not completely screened by trees look like illustrations from a freshly printed encyclopaedia of every architectural style since the Minoan civilisation. Factory-fresh limousines and replicars are parked in the open, so that the sun can light them up.

Even the most visible of these houses, however, is equipped to resist uninvited entry. Here the name Charles Manson is no joke. Gates have guard-houses and electric locks. There is closed-circuit television in the shrubbery. Lawns have spring-up spikes like a Vietcong ambush. These defensive measures should be kept in mind when you lay out two dollars for MAP AND GUIDE TO THE FABULOUS HOMES OF THE STARS and discover that ELKE SOMMER lives at 510 N BEVERLY GLEN, BEL AIR. Try walking in on her unannounced and you are likely to be greeted by an anti-tank missile coming down the driveway at chest height.

By now it was time to stop, before I became like the dazed heroine of Joan Didion's marvellous novel *Play It As It Lays* – the girl who drives on the freeways endlessly. We came home to Hollywood along Sunset Strip, which is really just a stretch of Sunset Boulevard that has let down its hair, not to say trousers. For a few strident blocks, THE ONLY TOTALLY NUDE LIVE STAGE SHOW ON THE STRIP vies for custom with MALE EXOTIC DANCERS. As S.J. Perelman deathlessly put it, De Gustibus Ain't What Dey Used To Be.

Blotto from having driven most of the day, we arrived back at Vidal's house to find a gigantic white Bentley clinging to the near-vertical driveway. Dudley Moore had come to assess the Yamaha piano for tone and tune. In England he used to drive a blue Maserati which he tended to leave undusted so that girls could write WE LOVE YOU DUD on the roof. He played beautifully then and he still plays beautifully now. High from having just seen the rough-cut of his new movie, he filled the evening air with sweet melancholy. Perhaps he was just delaying the tricky moment when he would have to back the Bentley down the driveway. It was like the launching of the Great Eastern.

Los Angeles might be impossible without a car but there is nothing to stop you going for a walk in Hollywood itself. There are footpaths, traffic lights and other useful pedestrian aids. It is true that William Faulkner once got arrested for walking but that was at night. Hollywood Boulevard is a good place to go in search of breakfast. The Chinese Theatre is still there, with the stars' names and handprints frozen into the cement outside the foyer. The handwriting is almost invariably huge and illiterate, like a child's drawings, while the handprints are the true signature. The movie industry was built by people who came up from nowhere.

Despite rumours to the contrary, the studios have never stopped growing. Most of the television programmes that stop people going to the movies are made in the movie studios. All television ever did was shrink the demand for ordinary movies. The demand for extraordinary movies increased. If any one thing is wrong with the movie industry today, it is the unrelenting effort to astonish.

The standard tour of Universal Studios is well worth the trouble. The place was a chicken farm when Carl Laemmle took it over in 1912. Now Universal City has 470 acres of tight-packed production facilities, including a back lot through which your tour tram climbs, dives and tunnels, while houses burn around you and bridges collapse beneath you. The tour is unflaggingly cute. I would have liked to have spent more time in the props warehouse, where five million props are classified in racks and shelves. Instead we had to watch a demonstration of the superhuman powers allegedly wielded by Six Million Dollar Man and Bionic Woman, both of whom stem from Universal. So does the Incredible Hulk.

So, once, did the Creature from the Black Lagoon, who used to emerge from one of the ponds on the back lot and press his rubberised attentions on Julie Adams. From *Frankenstein* and *Dracula* through to *Jaws* and *Battlestar Galactica*, Universal has always been a hot studio for monsters and special effects. I enjoyed my tour but often felt that I might as well have gone to Disneyland.

So I went to Disneyland. Fleeing south-east on the Santa Ana freeway, the Cadillac ate the miles. The sun was bright and once again there was stock-car racing taking place all around us. A topless Volkswagen Beetle with a Chevrolet V-8 motor and wheels off an F1 racing car went past us like a low-flying aircraft, its driver scanning the sky for police helicopters. The freeways distort time and space to the point where Disneyland, when you arrive, seems like reality. Hector and Alphonse knew the place inside out. They pronounced Pirates of the Caribbean to be the best ride.

Bobbing in a boat through tunnels and caves, you pass

through mock sea-battles and watch mock towns being mock sacked. Mock pirates chase mock wenches. What will happen to the wenches when they are caught? The question is never asked. Totally innocent purpose is combined with infinitely elaborate execution. In the Haunted Mansion the hologram ghosts sing and dance around the graveyard while a hologram severed head speaks to you from inside a crystal ball. The technology is post-Einstein, the psychology preteen. There is a connection: only a thumb-sucker could ever have dreamed such things were possible.

Hector and Alphonse persuaded me that without a ride on the Matterhorn my life would be incomplete. The Matterhorn is a high-speed switchback that loops around, when not hurtling through, an artificial mountain. Strapped into a drop-tank capsule I tried to think of other things while the G-force successively pushed my head through my collarbone, pulled it out again, and turned it back to front. Miraculously my Mickey Mouse ears stayed on, but I didn't dare open my eyes, lest something worse than what I was imagining was taking place. When I finally drummed up the courage to take a look, we were heading back in the Cadillac for dinner at Carlos and Charlie's on Sunset Strip. Plastic ears humming in the wind, I was ready for the heavy action.

June 16, 1979

Postcard from Los Angeles

2 Even with Uncle's Dogs

CREWED by my boy assistants Hector and Alphonse, the canary-yellow 1964 drop-head Cadillac delivered me at Carlos and Charlie's restaurant on Sunset Strip. The doorman looked askance at the Mickey Mouse ears which I had acquired at Disneyland and forgotten to take off. Airily I removed them and tossed them behind me into where the car would have been if the car-hop had not already driven it away. Carlos and Charlie's is currently one of the fashionable places to eat, if you discount the fact that by the time you have heard that a place is fashionable it isn't fashionable any more. It doesn't matter anyway. Good food is plentiful in Los Angeles. If you want to gawk at movie stars, you can always go to the movies.

Carlos and Charlie's specialises in Mexican food. Presumably Carlos looks after the kitchen while Charlie counts the money. Mexican cuisine places a lot of emphasis on the heat factor. You take a hot tortilla, drop it, pick it up, fill it with assorted meats, top if off with various hot sauces, roll it tight, and bite one end of it while the contents fall out of the other end into your lap. Hector and Alphonse introduced me to a pepper called the jalapeño. No bigger than your little finger, it just lies there innocently like a failed gherkin, but it goes off in your mouth like a petrol bomb. I thought the sun was coming up in my throat. Citizens of Mexico who accidently eat a jalapeño plunge immediately into the Rio Grande and swim to the United States, slowed down only by the drag of their open mouths.

After I had been put out with foam I was loaded into the

back of the Cadillac and driven through forests of neon to a disco called Osko's. The Cadillac drew narrow looks of appreciation from the car-hops. But they still parked it around the back instead of positioning it prominently near the front door alongside the Rolls-Royces and Mercedes which had been chosen for that honour. Style counts, but the house has its prestige to think of. Hector and Alphonse bought the Cadillac from an outfit called RENTAWRECK for less than the price of a new Mini. Cheap is cheap no matter how you polish it.

Osko's was full of dark sound fighting to get out. Tiny bulbs set into narrow slits in the floor lit up in sequence, chasing one another like particles in an accelerator. An amplified combo stamped out a trip-hammer beat at a volume calculated to burst John Travolta's pimples. You didn't have to dance. The floor danced for you. It was on springs. Ladies were not allowed to wear open-toed shoes, lest their writhing partners descend from shoulder-height and flatten a pedal digit into something that could be presented in court as evidence of negligence on the part of the management. But at least ladies were allowed to wear shoes of some kind. In almost every disco except Osko's what you have to wear is roller skates. Cher Bono and other stars have their own roller disco every Monday night: Jon Voight is supposed to be the greatest thing on eight wheels. Tomorrow roller-skates will give way to skis.

Then it was tomorrow. In my motel, the Casa Nervosa, the TV set woke me up to tell me that Captain Video was dead. In the 1950s I had seen every episode of *Captain Video*, a movie SF serial with such a low budget that the hero and the heavy shared the same spaceship, only the nose and tail being switched to indicate the change of owner. Captain Video had been played by Al Hodge, who later on, as the newsreader put it, 'had trouble getting parts'. Hodge had been found dead in a motel. Nobody came to claim the body. The announcement was a momentary acknowledgment of inexorable fate. Such lapses into gravity are uncommon in a city where the usual idea of tragedy is the hideous prospect of paying a dollar a gallon for gasoline.

Ever since Lana Turner was discovered engaged in the construction of a banana split, it has been axiomatic that any actor can get the big break. All she or he has to do is be in Los Angeles. The result is that most of the world's actors are in Los Angeles. Actresses who take jobs as waitresses are far more likely to find themselves waiting on other actors than on producers. The actors will have their heads buried in magazines like *Casting News*, whose Actors' Advice Column is hosted by Dennis Lamour. Q: IF I'M IN A SCENE HOW CAN I DO A GOOD JOB IF THE OTHER PERSON DOESN'T RELATE? ISOLATED, L.A. *Dear Isolated: Use their impenetrability as a catalyst for your character's underlying feelings. This could be anger, sadness, impotence, hatred, frustration, etc. A closed performance might mangle a scene, but your emotions, your work, your life, can still shine.* In Los Angeles there are thousands of Isolateds desperately trying to make their lives shine while the other person goes on not relating.

For the actress, while she is still young and looks good, there is always another way out. It isn't exactly theatre or the movies, but on the other hand it isn't exactly pornography. FEMALE ORIENTAL MODELS *eighteen and over are needed for nude figure modeling for European publications. No porno. Experience not necessary. All sizes OK. Models will work directly with producers. Call Mr Pimpa,* (213) 462-3455. Working directly with producers could mean anything, but in this case it probably means what it says. As for Mr Pimpa, at least he's got a telephone number.

Down among the real pornography, names and addresses are harder to trace. For 50 cents I bought the entrée into the hard-core section of a big bookshop on Santa Monica Boulevard. The stuff on the racks had to be seen to be believed. Once seen and believed, it quickly numbed the senses. I found it more difficult than ever to understand Lord Longford's agitation when faced with evidence of the tawdriness of human dreams. My own reaction was an overwhelming desire to lie down on the floor and go to sleep. VIRGINS FOR THE CARDINAL. SLUT FOR THE CRUSADERS. SLAVE TO THE SADISTIC WOODSMAN. EVEN WITH UNCLE'S DOGS. NAZI FILE (*Forced to submit to the Nazi dogs!*) NAZI TORTURE SHACK.

Literature for male homosexuals varied in tone. At one end of the scale there were Gordon Merrick's 'stories of Pete and Charlie'. Shyly equipped with titles like *The Lord Won't Mind* and *One for the Gods* ('A novel of Charlie and Pete – once more and forever!') these featured pastel cover illustrations of clean-cut young men holding hands. At the other end of the scale naked bruisers in steel helmets and hob-nailed boots were jumping up and down on each other's faces. For studs, there were magazines showing prostrate ladies being penetrated at all points and attempting to indicate gratitude with their eyes.

It might sound like paradox-mongering to say so, but there is something innocent about the supposition that happiness can be found by gratifying the body's wishes. It is certain that misery is to be found by not gratifying them, but beyond that nobody except a child can be sure. The Angelenos seem sure, and therefore childish, but it must be admitted that they have good excuse. Living in the climate and circumstances of Eden, they can be forgiven for behaving as if Los Angeles were the only reality and the rest of the world a dream.

In that sense Los Angeles is the world's biggest provincial town. But the sophisticate's confident scorn tends to become muted with proximity. You can't be in town two days without feeling the urge to take better care of yourself, drink more orange juice, run five miles before breakfast, do something about that wilting bicep, live for ever. It is but a short step to your first face-lift. Suddenly it seems a crime to be unhealthy. In his enthralling book *Arnold: the Education of a Bodybuilder*, Arnold Schwarzenegger quotes Plato on the subject. 'Plato wrote that man should strive for a balance between the mind and the body.' There is something to it, even if you can't help wondering what Arnold's mind must look like if his body is balanced by it. Plato would have jumped out of his sandals at

93

the mere thought of a human being ever looking like Arnold –
i.e., like a brown condom full of walnuts.

To Stone Canyon for lunch with Ken and Kathleen
Tynan. It was through country like this that Philip Marlowe
drove Lindsay Marriott to his appointment with death in
Farewell My Lovely. The canyons were lonely in those days.
Now there is no real-estate left to sell. But there are still
plenty of trees. The Tynans served lunch *al fresco*. I eyed
the Mexican salad warily, in case a jalapeño should be
lurking incognito behind a lettuce leaf. But everything tasted
delicious. The soft breeze took the sting out of the sunlight.
The talk ranged far and wide. I could stand a lot of this. I
started to be a bit sorry about having to go home. It was
easy to see why the Tynans had settled in so well. It would
have been no use pointing out, for the hundredth time, that
what the London theatre needs more than anything else is
for Kenneth Tynan to go through it like an avenging
angel.

The awkward truth about LA is that although it dares you
to laugh at it, you can't. No free person can afford to mock
Los Angeles, since liberty is its primary impulse. Not even
Forest Lawn is beneath contempt. EVERYTHING AT TIME OF
SORROW. There are in fact two main Forest Lawns, one in the
Hollywood Hills and the other at Glendale. The one at
Glendale is the crazier. People of a literary turn of mind have
always found the place easy to satirise, principally because
the Builder had a unique touch with the English language. It
is hard to remain unmoved when reading the Builder's Creed
carved in immortal stone. FOREST LAWN SHALL BE A PLACE
WHERE LOVERS NEW AND OLD SHALL LOVE TO STROLL AND
WATCH THE SUNSET'S GLOW. Such prose shall turn the unwary
reader's bowels to water.

After your first few minutes in Forest Lawn you find
yourself solemnly vowing never to be seen dead there. Plainly
The Loved One was not a novel but a straightforward docu-
mentary. But before you pull your coat over your head and
run for the exit, you simply must see the 'Last Supper'

window. '*Located in the Memorial Court of Honour in the Memorial Terrace of the Great Mausoleum, this radiant stained glass re-creation of Leonardo da Vinci's masterpiece is shown with a dramatic narrative daily on regular schedules.*'

While the radiant stained glass re-creation waits patiently behind plush curtains, the dramatic narrative is imparted by a disembodied, sepulchral voice-over of teeth-rattling resonance. The dramatic narrative consists of a long and involved story about how Dr Hubert Eaton enlisted the talents of every glass-stainer in Europe. At first everything went well. But then there was a hitch. Three times the image of Judas refused to form. Dr Hubert Eaton was on the verge of scrubbing the whole deal. But then word came through from Europe. Judas had jelled! Iscariot was intact! The stained glass re-creation of Leonardo da Vinci's masterpiece was at last complete! At this point in the dramatic narrative the dramatic narrator pauses dramatically. The plush curtains roll back, revealing a stained glass re-creation before which Leonardo himself, were he still with us, could do nothing but set fire to his own beard in silent tribute.

The same chapel that houses the stained glass whatsit is also a repository for copies of almost every statue Michelangelo ever carved. Before being outraged, you need to take stock of what you are being outraged at. The copies are micrometrically perfect. Only their clean finish serves to distinguish them from the originals. What *is* ridiculous is the way they have been torn from their historical context and placed in another context which has no history at all. To see sculptures by Michelangelo lovingly deployed against a background of such transcendental hideousness is enough to make you burst out crying. But what kind of tears? In part they are tears of annoyed envy that anybody could combine so much technical know-how with so much crassness. What incenses you is the airy thoroughness with which the old world has been plundered of its images and left behind. Forest Lawn is the clearest proof that Los Angeles is the whirlpool of the world, a geopolitical jacuzzi, a maelstrom in which all the styles and cultures have come to drown in one another's arms.

Nobody can defy death and stay sane. The biggest tombs in Forest Lawn house the embalmed corpses of plastic surgeons who got rich by encouraging people in the mad belief that time can be stopped. Yet in Los Angeles even that delusion becomes understandable. Life is so good that nobody wants to leave. The hidden assumption behind all the mockery that has ever been aimed at California is that existence is not meant to be that easy. The sophisticated Europeans who were exiled to Los Angeles – Stravinsky, Schoenberg, Brecht, Renoir, Ophuls and scores of others not much less exalted – often sneered at their new life, or other people sneered on their behalf. But in the countries they came from they would have been doomed, and in the place they had come to was a new energy. It was vulgar, but new energy always is.

By now the scornful visitor is a rarity. Europeans react with open admiration. John Boorman making *Point Blank* and David Hockney painting bigger and better splashes are only two examples of British artists responding to stylistic chaos with vigour instead of condescension. Even more indicative, the New Yorkers, once so quick to scoff, are becoming increasingly slow to go home. In the 1930s it was taken for granted by the writers from back East that they came to Hollywood only under financial duress; that what they wrote would be travestied before it reached the screen; and that their lives would be distorted if they stayed too long. Dorothy Parker, S.J. Perelman and the other New York wits never thought of veiling their contempt. Robert Benchley lamented his screen successes. But Scott Fitzgerald talked himself into a love affair with the studio system and in *The Last Tycoon* celebrated the very forces that helped destroy him.

Fitzgerald was romantic but it was he, and not the realists, who got it right. Despite all its absurdities, the movie industry really was as important as it thought it was. Even more important, Los Angeles was not going to go away. Since the war, during which the economy of California doubled all over again, everything not nailed down has come West. Johnny Carson's *Tonight* show, which initially was based in New York, came to LA each year for its annual holiday. In 1974 it forgot to go home. When the Dodgers sock the ball out of the park, it lands in Los Angeles, not in Brooklyn.

On my last night in LA I dined with Joan Didion and her husband John Gregory Dunne at their house in Pacific Palisades. His-and-hers twin Toyotas stood nose to nose in the driveway. Mexican food was served. Both writers unashamedly thrive in Los Angeles. Dunne's excellent long article about California in *New West* for January 1, 1979 is an unbroken paean, while even Didion's famously mordant title essay in *Slouching Towards Bethlehem* is written more from fascination than from fear.

Both writers make their money from writing movies and use the money to buy time in which to write their books – a system pioneered by William Faulkner. Both writers know in advance that scripting the remake of *A Star Is Born* for Barbra Streisand must inevitably entail a certain literary contribution by Ms Streisand herself. They know exactly what the difference is between compromise and capitulation. If two people so intelligent can live in Los Angeles on their own terms, then the place has become civilised in spite of itself. I enjoyed their company very much and did my best not to let them know that I had swallowed a jalapeño. They probably thought my muffled sobs were due to homesickness.

At midnight Hector and Alphonse fetched me away up through the hills to Mulholland Drive. From a look-out high on the ridge I could see all the way down the coast to Balboa and inland to the Sierra Madre. Turning around, I could see the whole of the San Fernando Valley. It was all one sea of light. This is where the first space voyagers will come from. When our children leave the Earth and sail away into relative time, they will have the confidence of naïvety. They will have forgotten what it is like not to get anything you want just by reaching out. In a way the Angelenos have already quit

America. Suddenly I felt compelled to see more of the land they have left behind. In the morning I cancelled my flight to London and caught the train for New York.

June 17, 1979

Postcard from Salzburg

A T THE Heathrow Terminal 2 check-in counter I was behind a 6 foot 6 inch male Ethiopian lacrosse goalie who had turned up three days early for a flight to Stockholm. It gradually became apparent that either he lacked the concept conveyed by the English word 'early' or else he thought that the girl behind the counter was threatening him with circumcision. An Australian on the way to Salzburg, I shared his unease.

Salzburg is in a part of Austria which could not be more mountainous without hitting the aeroplane. There are Alps everywhere. Dropping from the sky by courtesy of an Austrian Airlines Boeing 727, I surveyed a landscape straight out of *The Sound of Music*, that epic musical in which Julie Andrews and a small choir of yodelling siblings sing madrigals at the Gestapo, thereby rendering them helpless. Much of the film was in fact shot in this very area. Many a time in the next few days I was to see lush green slopes set at the precise angle for Julie Andrews to sprint up them and achieve lift-off.

The *Salzkammergut* winds through this precipitous area like a hidden valley, or rather a network of hidden valleys. The road from the airport tunnels through solid rock. *Salzkammergut* means salt chamber possession, an indication of what the valley's chief export used to be in ancient times. The glaciers carved steep walls. When they melted they left a string of lakes and fast-flowing rivers which cut the salt chamber still deeper. The strange wealth that made meat last longer was easy to get at. On the other hand the valley itself was not.

Under the old Roman Empire, the Holy Roman Empire that came later and the Austro-Hungarian Empire that came later still, the salt chamber always seemed to be by-passed by the hungry armies. Even the Thirty Years War hardly touched it. True, 20,000 Protestants were slung out after the mandatory tortures, but no armies came in. Napoleon went around instead of through. Hitler was born just over the hill, near Linz. Berchtesgaden, although high up, is so close by that Julie Andrews could reach it on foot in a matter of minutes. Yet Hitler's chief creation, the Second World War, left the district almost unharmed.

Salzburg's river is called the Salzach and still flows so fast over its rocky bed that it looks like a crowd of whirlpools running downstairs in a panic. Defined by the walls of the gorge and some eminently fortifiable outcrops, only one good place offered itself in which to build a town, and there they built Salzburg. It didn't, of course, happen all at once. For a long while after the Romans went away hardly anything happened at all. Then, during the long haul of the Middle Ages, the outcrops were found to be ideal places to build a fortress, a monastery and a convent. Snug in their separate walled residences, monks and nuns ignored the world and each other. Below the outcrops, churches and ancillary buildings accumulated on the flat stone shelves of the river-banks. The town became a little religious kingdom, ruled by whoever could get himself elected to the plush appointment of *Erzbischof* (Archbishop).

Supposedly these heavily ordained big-wigs wielded power on the Pope's behalf, but increasingly they were in business for themselves. Handing on the tall hat from one to the other, they tirelessly effected improvements, until the town graduated from a hole-in-the-wall hideout for monkish culture to a Gothic capital city which somehow contrived to stay intact while the wars of the Reformation raged behind the next mountain but one.

Reformation and Counter-Reformation slowed down the Renaissance but could not stop it. Theophrastus Bombastus von Hohenheim, commonly known as Paracelsus, worked and died in Salzburg. The Salzburgers should give him more publicity than they do. Though a drunk with abominable manners, he marked the transition from alchemy to chemistry. He never discovered the philosophers' stone, but he did manage to come up with zinc. If he could have hung on for a few years more he might have been patronised by the first true Renaissance *Erzbischof*, Wolf Dietrich, who came to power in 1587 and initiated the stylistic upheaval which eventually transformed Salzburg into the glittering showcase of baroque architecture that it remains today.

Like the princely rulers of the Italian city states, Wolf Dietrich knew how to pick talent. Indeed several of the architects he hired were Italians, a tradition continued under his successors, Markus Sittikus and Paris Lodron. Under *Erzbischof* Johann Ernst Graf Thun, who ruled from 1687–1709, the process was brought to its *Höhepunkt*, or apex. Fischer von Erlach, who shares with Lukas von Hildebrandt the honour of giving half of Austria the unfailingly ebullient look of the Catholic baroque, moved into town and started rapidly assembling masterpieces. The *Dom* and the *Kollegienkirche* are only two of his contributions. Hildebrandt barely got a look in. When the dust of construction settled, Salzburg stood revealed as a dream made actual – a miniature capital as beautiful as Cambridge, or as Dresden must have been before the fire-storm.

Erzbischof Firmian was the plug-ugly who organised the forced emigration (*erzwungene Emigration*) of the aforementioned 20,000 Protestants. Homogeneous once more, the Salzburgers gracefully stagnated. The rococo passed them by. The only thing that happened was the birth of a prodigiously gifted son to *Erzbischof* Schrattenbach's assistant *Kapellmeister*. As well as changing the entire world for the better, the advent of Wolfgang Amadeus Mozart came as close as anything in recent times to modifying the static perfection of Salzburg's architecture. Every second building now sports an elaborate plaque identifying it as the site of his birth, or of his wife's sister's death, or of his mother's brother's nephew's friend's dachshund's first litter.

Mozart's departure, which occurred not long after his arrival, was the last event for a long time. During the nineteenth century, Salzburg's main achievement was to become, at long last, part of Austria. Meanwhile, boredom thinned the population by 75 per cent. Salzburg was becoming an empty theatre. In the late teens of our century, Richard Strauss, Hugo von Hofmannstahl and Max Reinhardt found a way of filling it. With only the occasional interruption, the Festival has been growing ever since, until today it is almost big enough to contain the ego of its current prime mover, *das Wunder* Herbert von Karajan.

'*Der Chef kommt!*' ('Here comes the chief!') Blasting out of the sky in his private jet, arriving at the *Grosse Festspielhaus* in a succession of fast cars, von Karajan sets the tone of the Salzburg Festival. It's serious, it's highly organised, and above all it's expensive. Tickets for this year's new production of *Aida*, conducted by *der Chef* personally, had a face value of £100 plus and changed hands at up to $1,000 each on the night. For that price, if I had the money, Aida would have to sing like an angel, wear the Star of Africa in her navel and look like Catherine Deneuve dipped in truffle sauce. Is even von Karajan worth it?

Kiri Te Kanawa says yes. Coached and conducted by *das Wunder*, she has had a triumph this year as the Countess in *Figaro*. Accompanied only by her husband and three attendant Austrian aristocrats, she managed to give her posse of adoring fans the slip and keep a lunchtime tryst with me at a secret restaurant in a lakeside village which must remain *namenlos* (nameless). Nervous lest an insanely jealous Bernard Levin should appear suddenly out of the cuckoo clock, I tried to crack her on the subject of von Karajan. The girl whose voice had just been described by the *Salzburger Nachrichten* as flowing in an undisturbed stream like pure oil (*'im ungestörten Strom wie reines Öl'*) told me to forget it: the man was all artist, humble under the flash, and singing for him had been the greatest experience of her career.

I consoled myself with the reflection that *la* Kanawa is notoriously nice. She won't, for example, say a word against that small army of fanatical admirers who follow her to every opening night anywhere in the world, so that every time the curtain goes up on a new production she sees the same faces. Two of them belong to a pair of rich American consultant anaesthetists – I dimly remember being told that one of them is called Gassman – who have been known to fight each other for the last seat on a plane to wherever she is appearing next. Whether these activities impede their performance as anaesthetists there is no way of knowing, especially if you are the patient.

Tickets for *Der Rosenkavalier* were available, but only on the black market. The trail led from a man who knew a man to another man who knew a hotel room in which yet another man, whom I shall call Herr Taut, crouched over a small pile of tickets. For only double the face value he was prepared to let me have one of these. I had the choice of paying him off in a large wad of Austrian schillings or a small gold ingot. I won't tell you which course I chose, except to say that when he opened the wall-safe to stash my contribution it looked like Fort Knox in there.

Alas, the performance was only so-so. The *Grosse Festspielhaus*, a modern creation, has a Cinemascope-shaped proscenium that no good designer could relish trying to fill. Substituting for Gundula Janowitz, who had gone sick, Gwyneth Jones sang a reasonably tuneful but far too unpoised Feldmarschallin. Yvonne Minton looked sensational as Octavian but was oddly immobile; Baron Ochs was a boor, which he is supposed to be, but a bore too, which he is not. Only Lucia Popp, the finest Sophie of our day, was up to the standard I had expected.

The production was poorly detailed. At the opening of Act I the absence of Octavian's boots, and the presence on the Feldmarschallin's head of a large blond switch, gave the impression that one of the lovers had undressed in the toilet and the other had been making whoopee while wearing a hairpiece. Though pleased to be there, I was not thrilled. Nor was the noise coming out of the orchestra pit anything to write home about. After all, my musical standards for this magic work had been set by the old EMI album, on which Schwarzkopf heads the cast and the baton is brandished by von Youknowwho.

Still, the audience was a show on its own. We all looked very pleased with ourselves. The men wore the black ties of forty-seven different countries while the women appeared to have cornered the world's supply of Givenchy originals. With a face as beautiful as a blank cheque, Gunther Sachs floated by, his haunted eyes focused on the eternal challenge of trying to spend his income faster than it accumulates.

After the performance the thing to do is to dine at the *Goldener Hirsch*, Salzburg's most expensive hotel. Salzburgers always dine after the opera. They also dine before it. In fact they dine throughout the day. There is a meal in the middle of the morning to help ease the pangs of the long hiatus between breakfast and lunch. There are comparatively few meals in the afternoon but things pick up towards evening. A few decades of eating on that scale leaves the average Salzburg citizen with legs like Roscoe Tanner's – four beer barrels arranged in stacks of two. The men look even tougher.

The *Hirsch*, though an ideal spot for watching café society in action, is a hellishly expensive place to eat. The manager, Count Johannes Walderdorff, is careful to include a pauper's dish in every course, but you would need to be a fairly well-heeled pauper. Just out of town, at the *Seegasthof* Leopoldskron ('*ein architektonisches Juwel*'), his delightful mother courts bankruptcy by running a restaurant where the food is even better than at the *Hirsch* and costs almost nothing. You can eat in the open air while contemplating the baroque perfection of *Schloss* Leopoldskron across the lake. Max Reinhardt used to throw parties there. The building is almost as well-preserved as Gunther Sachs and costs a lot less to look at.

Salzburg can fall within the bounds of financial possibility if you pick, choose and plan ahead. There is no point raging against the price of festival tickets. They would cost three times as much again if the city and the State were not subsidising them. Unfortunately none of these reflections helps much when there is a performance of *La Clemenza di Tito* coming up and the house is sold out.

The lovely English mezzo Anne Howells was one of the principal singers in *La Clemenza* and slipped me a complimentary ticket. How, you might ask, did this come about? When I was a graduate student at Cambridge, Miss Howells appeared as a guest star to sing Béatrice in the Opera Society's production of Berlioz's *Béatrice et Bénédict*. I myself appeared in the non-singing but crucial role of a comic waiter who dropped plates. My performance was greeted with roars of indifference. Even today people who were in the audience still don't talk about it. For some reason my operatic career failed to take off. Miss Howells has gone on to greater things but she is not the sort of girl to forget a fellow artiste fallen by the wayside.

La Clemenza, or *Titus* as it is known locally, proved to be an excellent production – the kind of thing that gives a music festival its reason for existence. Mozart would have been pleased at the way James Levine's conducting gave his *opera seria* the appropriate gravity without sacrificing its tingling lilt. Queueing up either to murder Titus or else to implore his forgiveness, or both, the ladies, even when dressed as men, sang with unfaltering lyricism and dramatic bite. A subtle evocation of what ancient Rome must have looked like through the eyes of King Leopold II of Bohemia, the production, surprisingly enough, was by Jean-Pierre Ponnelle, who once perpetrated a television version of *Madame Butterfly* which left me undecided whether he should be fed to a small school of large sharks or a large school of small ones. But this time he had got it right.

Above all he was in the right theatre. The *Felsenreitschule*, as its name implies, is built into the cliffs. The back of the stage is a set of arcades carved long ago into the living rock. Hence the whole stage spectacle reflects the look of the city, in which streets like cliffs are punctured by alleys like caves. *Titus* is among Mozart's last works and this production fittingly matched the height of his career to the city of his birth. Even the audience caught the mood. During the interval people talked about Mozart instead of eyeing one another's clothes. Everybody liked everybody else. The Austrians even smiled at the Germans, which is saying a lot, because on the whole the Austrians would rather that the Germans just stayed home and sent the money by post.

Year after year Mozart comes home to Salzburg in triumph. You would think that he had flourished there. In fact he suffocated. Schrattenbach's successor as *Erzbischof* was a hard case called Colloredo, who gave the Mozarts a thin time. Wolfgang dreamed of getting out. Finally he had to beg permission. There is a letter from Mozart to Colloredo dated August 1, 1777 that is so full of honorific forms of address it reads like a German translation of a Japanese court circular. (*'Gnädigster Landes Fürst und Herr Herr!'*) Under the marmalade, Mozart's drift is that he yearns for Vienna. Despotism was too narrow a context for what the great musicians now had to offer. Mozart continued the small but significant political movement which began with Haydn and was to culminate in the symbolic moment when Beethoven crossed Napoleon's name off the Eroica, having realised that the truly free man was not the Emperor but he himself.

And even if Colloredo's despotism had been benevolent, Mozart would probably still have left Salzburg. Looking at the place, you wonder how any artist could want more. But Mozart had no need of perfect surroundings: he took such things in at a glance. For him, the only inexhaustible source of interest was the human spirit. Goethe was impressed with the King of Naples' dignity. Mozart noticed the way the King stood on a box to be taller than his Queen. Mozart could never falsify the variety of life, not even to the extent of exalting art above the mundane.

Salzburg is not Aldeburgh or even Edinburgh. Nothing much gets created there. Instead, it is an art-shrine. Karajan is the last *Erzbischof* of Salzburg. A Teutonic pall of *Kunst-begeisterung* (art devotion) would hang over the whole city if it were not for the Austrians' cheery dedication to the promptings of the flesh, especially those generated by a partly empty stomach. In Salzburg the portraits of the artists stare from every shop window. Countless von Karajans profile dramatically. Even Mozart, who had a sharp sense of his own worth and no fondness for being placed below the salt, would gag at so much worship. But the Austrians don't just put his portrait in the window. They wrap it around a globular blob of chocolate called a *Mozartkugel*. They make sugar busts of him. They eat him.

Yet even when awash with Festival kitsch Salzburg remains an enticing part of the historical accident which has left post-war Austria free, democratic and prosperous. Salzburg's idea of political unrest is a neo-Nazi demonstration with eight participants, seven of them from out of town. The police went into action. (*Trat die Polizei in Aktion.*) Count Octavian Rofrano has married Sophie. The aristocracy and the bourgeoisie have made a truce and the common people flourish in service of both. High on the valley walls, mist curls like liquid oxygen off the pines. The sails of the wind-surfers make triangular spectrums on the *Mondsee* at sunset. Small baroque clouds soak the green slopes with fine rain. Who is that dirndl-clad figure sprinting heavenward?

There was more to see but I had run out of time and cash. Going home to London I had to change planes in Zurich because Kiri Te Kanawa was booked on the only direct flight and the anaesthetists had bagged the last two seats.

October 21, 1979

Postcard from Paris

THE FIRST time I ever went to Paris was in the spring of 1963 and I was riding in the back of Charlie's van. The back of his van was open to the sky. It was full of blatantly English furniture Charlie had bought cheap around London and planned to sell dear in the Paris flea-market. He told the customs men at Calais that his French great-aunt had finally dropped off the twig in Chipping Sodbury and that it was time for her furniture, which was all French anyway – note these characteristic inlays – to come home to Paris. After all, was such furniture not part of *le patrimoine* – the patrimony?

This was definitely the magic word. We were waved through with no questions asked and a few hours later, as I stood leaning on a jolting rosewood military chest of drawers, we crested a hill and I got my first look at the City of Light. It was pastel blue. The Eiffel Tower was still the tallest building in Paris and looked so *chic* it made you laugh. I hammered on the roof of the driver's cabin and pointed straight ahead. Charlie nodded and blew the horn.

Charlie and I fell out subsequently. With my earnings from the Paris trip I rented a barge he owned that was moored at Twickenham. I was fully installed before finding out that the toilet, instead of emptying itself into the bilges, emptied the bilges into my kitchen. But that's another story, and anyway I have never ceased to be grateful to him for showing me that Paris belongs to anybody. You don't even have to speak the language. All you have to do is use your eyes. The patrimony is all there in front of you.

Whether it will be there much longer is a separate question. My latest trip to Paris took place last month. The aircraft was a European Airbus. Nobody except small boys and the men who built it knows who built it. As far as I remember from the brochure, the tail is made in Germany, the nose in Belgium and the ash-trays in Stockport. The airbus landed somewhere within the precincts of Charles de Gaulle airport at Roissy. A rotary milking machine with pretensions to elegance, Charles de Gaulle airport has by now spent several years being the ultra-modern gateway to Paris and like most ultra-modern buildings it shows early signs of becoming dated. The long travelators carry you more slowly than you want to go. One fainting old lady can gum up the entire works. You never get to see the aircraft you have just got off or indeed the aircraft you are about to get on. Charles de Gaulle airport is alienationsville. It is every nightmare Jacques Tati ever had come true.

Driving into Paris from the airport, you pass the tower blocks at la Défense. They are tall and nasty. There was a time not long ago when if you stood between the spread wings of the Louvre and looked along the axis linking the Tuileries, the Place de la Concorde and the Champs-Élysées, the line of sight ended at the Arc de Triomphe. Now the towers of la Défense are behind and above it, wrecking the scale of what used to be monumental.

Monumentality has more to do with proportion than with size. Haussmann's city planning, carried out between 1852 and 1870, has aroused plenty of hatred since. He based his layout on political requirements. The idea of the wide, straight boulevards was to provide the shortest unbarricadable route between the barracks and the likeliest source of trouble – where the workers lived. Everything else was just decoration, some of it pompously massive by the standards of the intimately scaled buildings that were mown down to make way for it. But judged by what has been allowed to happen recently, Haussmann's Paris looks delicate.

Checking into my hotel in the Rue de Seine, on the Left Bank between Boulevard Saint Germain and the river, it occurred to me that I had moved up in the world. There was a pillow. Whenever I was in Paris during the Sixties – and it was never often enough, alas – I could afford only the kind of hotel where they gave you what felt like a rolling-pin wrapped in calico. You could bash yourself over the head with this in hopes of rendering yourself dizzy enough to get some sleep on a bed that resembled a ping-pong table without the flexibility. There used to be a jug of cold water standing in a bowl. You poured the water into the bowl, spread some of it upon your person, dried yourself with a towel which had previously seen service as a bandage during the days of the Commune, and pronounced yourself clean.

Too old now for such discomfort, I have still not lost my loyalty to the 5th and 6th *arrondissements*. The Latin Quarter still strikes me as the most hospitable place in the world for someone who likes to buy books, sit around and read them, or even write them. As long as that one small area remains unreconstructed, Paris will still have its heart. But even that area is already desperately short of Parisians. With an apparent inexorability which has been movingly described by Richard Cobb in a brilliant series of articles for *The Times Literary Supplement* and the *New York Review of Books*, most of the ordinary people who used to live and work in central Paris have been forced out to the deadly Alphaville housing developments of the periphery.

But at least in the Latin Quarter the houses they have left behind are still lived in. The middle class has taken over. In the Rue de Seine street-market, most of the ladies doing the shopping look like Edwige Feuillère at the height of her career. Gentrification makes the visitor feel relaxed: perhaps because, though it is an illusion, it is the same illusion which waits for him at home. A further side-effect is that the physical fabric of the affected area is jealously preserved.

There are not many visitors in the depth of winter but café life thrives anyway. People sitting in the glass-fronted cafés of the Boulevard Saint Michel and the Boulevard Saint Germain are there for you to look at as you walk past, just as you are there for them to look at as they sit sipping. As of old, some cafés are in and others are out. The Coupole, on the Boulevard Montparnasse, is the place to be for Sunday lunch. The clientele is literary and the crêpes are a pale-blue bonfire. The Coupole's legend is still current. Other Montparnasse cafés now belong to the glorious past: the Dôme, the Sélect, the Closerie des Lilas. Hemingway used to come sprinting by on tip-toe, just ahead of the crowd. It wasn't long ago.

This whole spectacle, one of the longest-running shows on earth, is made possible by the width of the footpath. Walter Benjamin, a precursor of Professor Cobb in the scholarly love of Paris, was particularly illuminating on this aspect. He wrote a fascinating essay on how the lay-out of Paris determines its creative life. As a Marxist, Benjamin condemned Paris for being the capital city of the bourgeois nineteenth century, but as a German Jewish intellectual he obviously loved every street of it.

In Paris Benjamin could be what he was – a cosmopolitan. Chesterton, who didn't like cosmopolitans, said that a great city was a place to escape the true drama of provincial life and find solace in a fantasy. What Chesterton didn't consider was that there is sometimes no other way of discovering yourself. For a long time now, artists of every kind have come to Paris in order to realise their true natures. Usually their true natures turn out to be unremarkable and they either stay on as fringe-dwellers or else go home again. But sometimes the self-discovery shakes the world.

Picasso was a case in point. An important Picasso exhibition was in its last days, so I hurried along. The Pont des Arts is closed for repairs so I crossed the river at the Pont du Carrousel and turned left through the Louvre into the Tuileries, which are at their second best on a winter's day. They are at their best on a misty spring morning, but if you cannot have that, then seeing them frozen stiff will do at a pinch. The leafless branches look like glass nervous systems in the blue air, through which the sleet falls as if the whole scene were being stage-managed by Pissarro. What Pissarro left out, needless to say, was the way it feels to have a small cone of white slush on top of your head.

Picasso's personal selection from his own best things, the

800 works on exhibition had been received by the State in lieu of death duties. (*Oeuvres reçues en paiement de droits de succession.*) They thus formed a crash course in Picasso's idea of his own artistic odyssey. Homeric similes sprang naturally to mind, since the queue to get in was already an epic. While standing outside in the cold there was plenty of time to notice how the view across the extravagant Pont Alexandre III to the Invalides has been intruded upon by the Montparnasse Tower, a skyscraper of an altitude which would satisfy even Colonel Seifert's cloud-piercing criteria. Whoever built that thing had an ego comparable with that of Napoleon himself. The Emperor is fortunate to be down a hole in the Invalides with seven coffins between him and the increasingly crenel-lated horizon.

The exhibition was so overpowering that I won't try even to list its highlights. By now, however, the philistines having decisively lost the battle, it might be possible, without being thought of as having joined their side, to venture a small doubt. Surely this is the endless inventiveness of a titanically gifted child, rather than a grown man? I have never liked Cubism much, and the transformations that came later I have never liked at all. *Picasso poursuit l'élaboration de ses formes* ... Yes, but in any other art the man who pursues the elaboration of his forms is soon given up as a dead loss. Another way of putting it would be to say that Picasso kept finding new ways of avoiding maturity.

We are supposed to feel inadequate for finding the Blue and the Rose periods consistently more beautiful than what followed. But they are consistently more interesting too, and what follows attains the same level of interest only when it gives up the intellectualised concern with pure form and momentarily pays attention again to the visible world. It is notable that this invariably happened, however briefly, when Picasso took a new mistress. Perhaps each of these lucky ladies simply insisted on a few more-or-less straight portraits before he got going again with the pursuit of his forms. Anyway, there they are, shining out of the exhibition –

breath-taking images of Olga, Marie-Thérèse, Dora, Fran-
çoise and Jacqueline.

You can dislike nine-tenths of everything Picasso did and
still can't deny his genius. Perhaps it is a reflection on oneself
to find him babyish. But there is something more admirable,
as well as less frightening, about a steady ripening of the
faculties. I like the old hand who grows wise in his profession.
Degas always used to say that he was more interested in
talent at forty than in talent at twenty.

Walking back to the Louvre, I stopped in at the Jeu de
Paume. Degas is represented there by pictures both early
and late. I find his gradual but unfaltering liberation
into colour and space inspiring beyond expression. Among
Picasso's personal hoard of pictures by other artists – the
collection has recently been given a room of its own in the
Louvre – there are many drawings by Degas. Significantly
they are all brothel scenes and show plenty of tuft. This was
one aspect of Degas but it wasn't everything. For Picasso,
however, it *was* everything. In life he was foul to his children
because by growing up they reminded him that he would one
day die. In his art he was the weeping minotaur, forever
complaining about waning potency, as if creativity depended
on nothing but that. Degas knew better, perhaps because he
was more civilised. He was, after all, French.

Yet French civilisation stinks of blood. Just outside the Jeu
de Paume, in the Place de la Concorde, the heads rolled. The
most celebrated of the three guillotines set up under revolutionary auspices did its work here. During the Terror it
decapitated 1,343 victims, not counting Louis XVI – a good
half of the grand total of 2,600 people who died under the
nation's razor.

The tumbril used to start its journey at the Conciergerie on
the Île de la Cité. This time I at last nerved myself up to enter
its gates, but I can't pretend it was a pleasant experience.
You can still hear the voices. The poet André Chénier is said
to have shown great courage, but the man I admire most is
Camille Desmoulins. The guide books don't mention him,

which is a pity. He laughed at Saint Just's long face and paid the inevitable penalty. *C'est ma plaisanterie qui m'a tué.* ('My joke has killed me.') His fate would have been mine, if I had lived then and had been as brave.

Conquering snobbery, I took an excursion on one of those river boats that look like a greenhouse. The corny thing is usually worth doing. Sleet looks more amusing when there is a plexiglass roof to stop it hitting you. The bilingually vulgar guide was full of information. On the Île Saint Louis, for example, Chopin's old house is now occupied by Michèle Morgan. You can bet he would have liked her in *Quai des Brumes*. Chopin lived eighteen years in Paris and there wasn't a day he didn't long for Poland, but there was no going back. In Paris he could be himself, just as Aurore Dudevant could be herself – George Sand.

In Paris the Italian painter Modigliani had an affair with the Russian poet Anna Akhmatova. Modigliani died young, mainly from malnutrition. Akhmatova went on to become one of the inextinguishable symbols of Russian literature during the Soviet period. When the regime was vilifying her it always singled out her carefree years in Paris for particular execration. The regime was right. If freedom is what you hate, then eventually you must hate Paris.

But we are talking about the ideal Paris, the patrimony of all mankind. The Parisians can take less comfort in the eternal verities. For one thing, legends often work to destroy themselves. Paris has been such a success as a painters' town that there are no real painters left in it. I climbed Montmartre to find the square crammed with Japanese art students. The ambient temperature was enough to turn a hot pancake into a cold dishcloth in less than two minutes but still the Japanese flung paint undaunted.

They paint in Paris the way they ski in Japan. A Japanese ski slope is a tight lattice-work of crossed skis in which thousands of aspiring skiers stand motionless. Montmartre is a forest of easel-painters sitting shoulder to shoulder and tirelessly translating the scene before them into an Impressionist simulacrum. Since the scene before them is a forest of easel-painters sitting shoulder to shoulder, it will be appreciated that many of the resulting paintings show a certain monotony of subject.

From the steps of the Sacré-Coeur on Montmartre you can look down into Paris and see everything that has happened to it for hundreds of years. One of the things that has happened recently is the Centre Pompidou, which disfigures the Marais area as if a giant, rattletrap air-conditioner had been dropped from a sky-hook. But at least the Centre Pompidou, though fat, is not tall. It does not ruin the skyline and from close by it is not even easy to find. Once found, it makes you wish that it had stayed lost a bit longer. The general idea of the building is that it wears its insides outside. All the internal conduits are featured externally, arousing the fear that anything one contributes to the sewage system might reappear elsewhere in the building labelled as a work of art.

Once inside the outsized inside that lies within the inside-outside, I was disconcerted to find myself having a good time. Part of the fun was provided by the startling rate at which the building is already falling to pieces. Less astonishingly, a Dali retrospective was in progress. Faced with a virtually complete record of the old phoney's unswerving bathos, it was impossible not to burst out yawning. Occasionally his wife had persuaded him to paint her without a steak over one eye. (Her eye, that is: the steak over his eye presumably remained in place.) Apart from these few lucid moments the uproar of banality numbed the mind. Japanese art students stood dutifully scrutinising such masterpieces as 'Premature Ossification of a Railway Station'. But despite the pitiless tedium one's heart was light. The building is a good place to see paintings, even if they are by Dali.

If they are by Bonnard, Picasso or Klee – all represented in the permanent exhibition – then the Centre Pompidou becomes a real pleasure. All you have to do is remember the glumness induced by the Palais d'Art Moderne, a concrete temple from which I once stumbled vowing never to look at Léger again.

Of course it's easy for a visitor to decide that he quite likes, or doesn't entirely loathe, the Centre Pompidou. He doesn't have to live with it. The Parisians do, and there is a good case for saying that it will take only a few more such experiments to screw *le patrimoine* for keeps. But even at the current rate of change it will be some time before Paris is ruined for the visitor. I don't like the idea of being a mere visitor but can't pretend to be anything more exalted. To my lasting regret, I never lived that long stretch in the city which alone enables one to speak its language. Indeed I speak hardly a word of French. But I spend a lot of time reading it. I taught myself to read French out of Proust. It took years, and I ended up enthralled by him. Even more than Renoir's Paris or Baudelaire's Paris, Proust's Paris is between my mind and the real Paris.

Probably there is no real Paris, except if you have always lived there. For those of us who arrive only to go away, the place teems with ghosts. In the Champs-Élysées on a winter morning, the young Proust threw snowballs at Marie de Benardaky and already marvelled at how the girl he dreamed of was growing separate from the real girl. Thus it was that Gilberte began to live for ever.

Soon the Académie française will issue a new edition of the dictionary. It will be not much larger than the old edition. As far as culture can influence politics, the patrimony will be conserved. Whether any great city can remain unchanged for long has yet to be proved. While waiting for the proof, the visitor might as well see the sights. I spent the last evening of my stay at the Crazy Horse Saloon.

Apart from myself, the audience consisted exclusively of Japanese businessmen. When the lights went down it looked like a bad night on Iwo Jima. The curtains parted and a dozen cuties wearing nothing except platform boots and appendectomy scars started doing close-order drill while miming to play-back. Sporting such names as Vanilla

Banana and Trucula Bonbon, they proved conclusively that human flesh can look exactly like wax fruit in the right light. The ecstatic customers flashed their bridgework at each other and waited for the girls to land in their laps. It never happened and it never will, but it doesn't hurt to dream.

February 10, 1980

Postcard from Washington

B RITISH Airways Flight 191 to Washington was a Boeing 747 called *John Donne*. It will be recalled that Donne advised his congregation not to send to know for whom the bell tolls. This admonition crept into my mind when Flight 191 showed signs of developing a nervous twitch. 'We have one passenger too many,' said the public address system. 'Would any passenger who is not going to Washington please make himself known to the cabin staff.' Luckily Flight 191 had not yet left Heathrow, so the extra passenger, once identified, was able to leave the plane at comparatively low altitude. She was an Indian dwarf nun from Tel Aviv.

Once *John Donne* was at cruising altitude the public address system got back into action. 'The film we will be showing is *Kramer versus Kramer*. The story of a marriage breaking up this award . . . The story of a marriage breaking up, this award-winning movie stars Dustin Hoffman and Muriel Stirrup.' Having seen the movie already, I decided to read my schools' edition of Cicero's *Pro Murena*, as part of a self-imposed extension course designed to prove that there is nothing new under the sun. The Senate and the People of

Rome, I had deduced in advance, would be worth bearing in mind when I gazed for the first time on the white dome of a more recent Capitol.

By the time of our final approach to Washington the man on the public address system was definitely out to lunch. 'The temperature in Washington is twelve minutes past three in the afternoon.' When he said 'Next stop Dallas' I panicked completely, but this time it was my fault. I had misheard. What he had said was 'Next stop Dulles.' Washington's international airport is named after John Foster Dulles, a busy style-setter in America's post-war foreign policy who retired to an honoured grave and eventually metamorphosed into an airport.

Washington, when you finally get to it after a long drive through the woods, immediately strikes you as a beautiful city. On the way in you pass CIA headquarters but you don't notice, even though it is an eleven-storey building. This is because the building goes down into the ground instead of up into the sky. Washington proper happily reverses this tendency although not by much. Strict laws keep the buildings low. Yet the effect of the central public area is genuinely monumental, which tells you that monumentality has more to do with proportion than with sheer size.

My hotel was a few steps from the White House, so I dumped my bags and went walking. Even in the late afternoon the heat was crushing. But as always happens, no matter how often one visits America, the really overwhelming thing was the affluence. A black lady who is no doubt leading a deprived life went past in a dented car. But the car was a Cadillac and the dent was not very big. A delinquent-looking youth on roller skates hissed by, snapping his fingers in time to whatever was happening in his stereo headphones. The roller-skates were multi-coloured works of art. The streets, at least in this part of town, seemed impossibly clean in comparison to London. The public telephones were unvandalised. For a London telephone booth to look like that it would have to be guarded round the clock by the SAS.

My eyes quickly filled with sweat but luckily the lay-out of the central area is easy to grasp. It is like a kite, with the White House at the northern end of the cross-bar and the Jefferson Memorial at the southern end. At the nose of the kite, in the west, is the Lincoln Memorial, and at the tail end in the east, on a small hill known universally as the Hill, is the Capitol.

Displaced slightly from where the spine and cross-bar join, the Washington Monument spears straight up. It is not especially tall but because of the surrounding space it looks heroic. The same applies to the Capitol: the top of the Hill is only 88 feet above the Potomac but it is enough to give the building wings as well as weight.

The lay-out was planned by a French major of engineering called Pierre Charles L'Enfant after what he called 'much menutial search for an eligible situation'. The word 'menutial' is not to be found in any dictionary but it probably just means that he tried hard. Nowadays he lies buried in Arlington cemetery just across the river, doubtless brooding on how often his fair plan was fatally injured in the carrying out.

The monumental buildings each had separate architects – some of them more than one. Pennsylvania Avenue, L'Enfant's great projected road from the White House to the Capitol along the top long edge of the kite, was cluttered up from an early date and is only today being given the attention due to it. On each side of the Mall – the long grass boulevard between the Capitol and the Monument – there is a row of public buildings united only in their eclecticism.

Also the surrounding residential districts are not all as prosperous as Georgetown in the north-west. More than half the voting population are black people and where they live still bears the scars of the riots that followed the murder of Martin Luther King. On 14th Street at night there are enough whores, pimps and drug pushers to remind you that this is not Paradise.

Yet L'Enfant's original clarity of mind shines through, creating an impression of dignity matched by few other purpose-built capital cities on earth. Not even in Leningrad does the prospect before you give such a feeling of reasoned gravity, even though Leningrad is entirely free of joggers.

In Washington there are joggers everywhere. The working day starts early – the President and his staff are at their desks by eight in the morning, all set, some say, to do the wrong thing – but it is mandatory to jog beforehand. There is more jogging during the short lunch-break and then a really solid, vein-bursting long jog at the end of the day.

Joggers come pounding towards you from every angle. It is not like New York, where, according to Dick Cavett, everyone jogs in the same direction around Central Park except Jackie Kennedy, who jogs in the other direction in order to avoid publicity. In Washington the jogging is more individualistic, if that is the right word for something everybody does. As I walked among the trees near the Lincoln Memorial, a jogger burst out of the shrubbery, swerved on to the road, and started hurdling a row of barriers warning about men at work. The men were not actually working at the time because it was their lunch-hour and they were all away jogging.

President Carter jogs in the Rose Garden of the White House, away from the public eye, which has anyway already been sated with the vision of the Chief Executive collapsing from exhaustion during a mass jog and being carried off at the trot by a brace of Secret Service operatives. As I walked very slowly along through the heat, intermittently rocked in alternate directions by the slipstream of passing joggers, I wondered whether even de Tocqueville would have been capable of explaining present-day America. Is there any other country, even Japan, which places such emphasis on symbolic activity? Where else would middle-aged men run until their hearts gave out in the pursuit of health?

But it is usually a mistake to look for a secret before you have ruled out the possibility that there might be no secret. Washington lives for politics – indeed it has no other manufacture of any importance. It is a company town. Political life in Washington is notoriously a matter of all-consuming complexity. Residents of Washington are even keener than anybody else to believe that the real action happens behind closed doors.

And yet by Whitehall standards an astonishing amount takes place in public. After a night spent listening to the air-conditioning unit doing a brilliantly successful impersonation of a dishwasher, I took a cab out to the Hill. Cabs in Washington are cheap but you might have to share. You meet a lot of people that way and there is no problem about finding a topic of conversation. Invariably it is politics.

On the Hill I wandered into a sitting of a House Committee on Energy, chaired by a Democrat Congressman called Toby Moffett. An ex-Nader's Raider, Moffett is widely regarded as a coming boy. He is also widely regarded as Edward Kennedy's man. His committee's main aim, apparently, is to establish that the Carter administration's recommendations to the States about conserving energy have had no effect.

Such a hearing, if it ever took place in Whitehall, would not be open to the public, and even if it were it would be called off immediately once it was revealed that the investigators were pursuing their inquiries with the aid of internal memos secured from the department concerned by means unstated. But the automatic assumption here is that the public has the right to know, so nobody feels guilty about obtaining private memos from 'sources'.

In my position as visiting interpreter with a few hours' experience, it also occurred to me that Moffett's committee must be a large embarrassment to the President. Moffett belongs to the same party as Carter but his allegiance is to Kennedy, and if Moffett's committee manages to uncover yet another story of amiable bumbling by the boys from Georgia it will be of considerable help to Kennedy should he decide to run in 1984.

'It's a question of leadership,' Moffett kept saying. Whenever a Democrat mentions 'leadership' he is really talking about what Kennedy has that Carter hasn't. Was Moffett campaigning for Kennedy as well as pursuing the truth? I asked him this during a short break in the hearings and received a very nice smile about four inches across and an inch high.

The Sans Souci is where all the President's men hatched the Watergate cover-up. The menu is tastier than the food but there is a lot of *ambiance*, much of it generated by the waiters, who have worked hard on their French accents. There were frequent mentions of the vine Liszt, which turned out to be the wine list. But nothing could blunt the tang of history. At my very table Haldeman and Ehrlichman had sat with German haircuts locked together and worked at the task of subverting the United States Constitution, which states that a Presidential Party shall not be formed. The Founding Fathers were rigorous on that point. Always a Senate but never a Caesar.

Many European observers found it difficult at the time to realise why there was so much fuss in America about Nixon's petty crimes. In Russia or China, they correctly pointed out, such things happen every day. But one of the central points of the Constitution is that the administration's power shall not be exercised unwatched. Such concepts as Checks and Balances and the Separation of Powers are actualities, not shams. There is a limit to what the government of the day can do, and even then the Republican party is permanently dedicated to the proposition that the Government should do even less. Ronald Reagan, who lies down instead of jogging, thus fits the Republican presidential ideal rather better than one might imagine.

Heading back to the Hill that afternoon, I almost collided with the President's motorcade. He was back in town after a hard week on the campaign trail. I left the House Committees to get on with their various tasks and tried my luck with a Senate Committee. The first one I walked into was dealing with the issue now known to the world as Billygate.

In the famous Caucus Room, where both John and Robert

Kennedy declared their intention to run for President, the Attorney-General of the United States was being grilled by Strom Thurmond of South Carolina while lights blazed down and a score of TV cameras looked on. Thurmond kept referring to a man called Mr Tairney Jonnell. I spent some time wondering who Tairney Jonnell was before I realised that he meant the Attorney-General. 'Mister Tairney Jonnell, *wha* did yew make that phone coll?'

Mr Civiletti put up a spirited defence but plainly the whole affair had been mismanaged. Also plain was that Mr Brzezinski would eventually have to put in an appearance and that when he did he would have to listen to several things he didn't want to hear, prominent among which would be Strom Thurmond's pronunciation of his name. Whether politics ought to be like a television programme is a moot point, but nothing beats such scenes for making a television critic feel like a political reporter. It was getting easier to see why Washington journalists suffer such a high incidence of terminal head expansion. They are needed. The whole place thrives on publicity.

That evening I flew up to New York on the shuttle for dinner with the editors of the *New York Review of Books*. It was like leaving a small town for the big city. As the dipping sun lit the water silver we flew close to the West Side of Manhattan at the same height as the tops of the tall buildings and made a diving turn into La Guardia. With the marble dust of the Caucus Room still on my shoes I was in a cab on Park Avenue before dark. At dinner there was only one possible topic of conversation. The 43-year-old Youth Culture hero Abbie Hoffman, after six and a half years on the run, had decided to give himself up to ABC roving reporter Barbara Walters.

Nobody questioned that Barbara had a right to interview Abbie before the cops got him. The big interview was scheduled for that night. We saw Barbara journeying by speedboat to the pickup point. 'Hi Barbara.' 'Hi Abbie.' Abbie's face had been altered by plastic surgery but his mouth was still occupied with its favourite subject. 'I hear the name Abbie,' said Abbie, 'and I . . . ' Barbara nodded wisely.

A phone call to Alfred Friendly, Brzezinski's press secretary, yielded prompt results. Friendly, born and bred in Washington, told me to get the 7 a.m. shuttle back to town and meet him at the White House. 'Being on the 7 a.m. shuttle', said Friendly in a friendly fashion, 'shows you're really serious about Washington.' I dropped red-eyed out of the sky and Friendly ushered me inside. Behind closed doors at last!

Down underground where Brzezinski lives it looks exactly like the sets of *Blind Ambition* except that there are Russian theatre posters on the walls, betokening the fact that Zbig and his staff have high intellectual qualifications for the job. And indeed Friendly, though he had made me promise in advance to stay off grand issues, was inexorably drawn into a discussion of the world, America's place in it, and the place of the Carter administration in the history of modern US foreign policy.

In many ways, he argued, people are complaining about having been given what they asked for. Watergate has made it harder than ever for the President to get anything done, even supposing that there were an amenable coalition on the Hill, which there is not, and hasn't been since Johnson. Nevertheless there *has* been, in recent years, a clear improvement in the standard of information available to the President, even if he can't act on it. Washington is stiff with research institutes. This is some compensation for how security-conscious everyone has become. 'I grew up here when Dean Acheson and Felix Frankfurter walked to work from Georgetown. Harry Truman would leave the White House and walk around Washington, and journalists would sometimes get a story. Now it's a story if some Senator runs to work.'

The morning having worn on, it is now time for the President to take off for Camp David. Friendly waves me out to the back lawn, upon which a large helicopter sits whistling. Out of the White House strides the President, his walk as weird as Nixon's but his hair style unimpaired. Rosalynn is beside him and a team of aides is carrying golf clubs and fishing rods. This could be a way of telling the waiting hordes of media people that the President plans to spend the weekend playing golf and fishing.

The President's hairstyle safely inside, the helicopter spins its rotors. A mighty wind smites the lawn. Up he goes, and all our prayers go with him, for here truly is an act of faith, when you consider what happened to all those helicopters on the Iran mission.

The State Department occupies a large building called Foggy Bottom. With every new administration there is a mass influx of brilliant appointees, accompanied by a mass exodus of the old ones, who wave goodbye to the rented furniture in their Georgetown houses and go back to the universities. In fashionable Washington only the hostesses and the journalists are permanent.

Foggy Bottom is haunted by a particularly in-the-know species of journalist whose chief glory is to be first-named at daily briefings. I went to a daily briefing. Assistant Secretary of State George Tratner was answering, or rather not answering, questions. 'Are these reports about the Cubans in Afghanistan internal reports?' 'I wouldn't want to characterise them, Bernie. Let's call them reports.' 'Have PLO people gone to Nicaragua to train Nicaraguans on Eastern bloc weapons?' 'I don't have any information on that, John.' Bernie and John looked satisfied.

The Carter administration is unpopular with the Washington hostesses because the boys from Georgia can't find the time to attend dinner parties. But the hostesses can wait. They have always been there. In Lincoln's time their pretty daughters toured the Virginia battlefields and posed for photographs with the young officers. The average Washington hostess can still muster a dazzling table even if Hamilton Jordan's feet are not on it. The table tends to be beside a swimming pool on the back lawn of a Georgetown house that looks small from the front, but unfolds into a tastefully appointed mansion inside.

In just such a house I had the great privilege of watching the Miss America Pageant on television. Sponsored by Silk-ience Self-Adjusting Shampoo ('It beats the grease without beating the ends'), the contest was won by a small-town girl who convincingly sang a Menotti aria. 'For me,' she told the world, 'success is important, and can only be attained by keeping my feet firmly on the ground while reaching for the stars.' Some of our beauty queens have longer legs but fewer qualifications as opera singers. The show was hosted by the latest Tarzan. A very tall man with even shorter legs than the winner, he managed to smile and talk at the same time, a feat of strength which caused hair-line cracks to appear in his sun-tan. Nevertheless I was impressed with the air of striving which the programme exuded. The productivity of America never ceases to amaze.

Some of the results are in the Air and Space Museum, which I infested on Sunday afternoon. The Bell X-1 that Chuck Yeager flew through the sound barrier is hanging from the roof, and up there beside it is the Douglas Skyrocket that Scott Crossfield flew to Mach 2. In 1953 I used to collect photographs of the Skyrocket and paste them on my bed-room wall, so that I could lie there and imagine what it would be like to fly in something so beautiful. Seeing the actual machine nearly thirty years later gave me the same thrill. We should always remember that when the Americans talk about being in a slump, they mean a slump by their stan-dards. For the visitor, the sheer wealth of the country must always remain the abiding impression.

And how all that energy should be governed remains the abiding question. The best event of my trip happened on the last day when I met I.F. Stone, the greatest journalist ever to make Washington his beat. Still in fighting form at seventy-four, Stone has been for a good part of his life the conscience of America. He got at the truth not through being first-named by politicians or hanging around hostesses but by reading the Congressional Record. 'The virtue arose from necessity,' he explained. 'I'm so deaf that I can't hear what anybody says.'

Stone is a perpetual autodidact of staggering prowess. Delighted to find me reading Cicero, he took me through his classics library book by book – the most educational two hours I have ever spent. 'The biggest difference between ancient Rome and the USA,' Stone contended, 'is that in Rome the common man was treated like a dog. In America he sets the tone. This is the first country where the common man could stand erect. I prefer it that way, even though we have a leadership crisis right now. The country was in far worse economic shape in the Thirties, but the reason we didn't have Carter's famous malaise under Roosevelt was that we had more leadership.'

So there it is. If even such an acute analyst as I.F. Stone thinks the problem lies with Carter, the problem lies with Carter. But supposing a strong leader were something to be wished for, where would he come from? It is doubtful if Abraham Lincoln would submit himself to the modern electoral process. I went to visit him in the Lincoln Memorial. He wasn't saying anything, but two of his speeches were up on the walls: the Gettysburg Address and the Second Inaugural Address.

It is impossible to read such unadorned eloquence without a tightening of the throat. But some of his most penetrating remarks have never been carved in stone. One of them is in the Reply to a Serenade of November 10, 1864. 'It has long been a grave question whether any government not too strong for the liberties of its people, can be strong enough to maintain its existence in great emergencies.' Lincoln thought the trick could be worked, but he was a great man. With less great men in charge it begins to look as if we want more from America than it can give: we want it to be the embodiment of freedom, and we also want it to be firmly led, so that it will not frighten us with its unpredictability.

With only a few hours left I had barely enough time to begin being stunned by the National Gallery, which just on its own would have made the trip worth while. Then I walked down the Mall to the Washington Monument and turned north towards the White House. As the joggers steamed past me in the heat, the first big cold front of the fall was moving east across Montana. Soon the leaves would be browning southward at twelve miles a day. My plane and the first football of the new season left the ground at the same time. The Washington Redskins were at home to the Dallas Cowboys. Dallas, not Dulles.

September 28, 1980

Mrs T. in China

1 The Dragon Lady Flies East

IT WAS Wednesday in Peking. Out of a pale sky as delicately transparent as the finest *ch'ing-pai* ware of the Sung dynasty came the wolf-grey and sharktooth-white RAF VC-10 bearing the great British War Leader Margaret Thatcher and her subservient retinue.

The British Media, who were along for the ride, tumbled down the rear gangway and took up their positions in a tearing hurry, because the War Leader would be among the first of the official party to deplane. Hands in China have to be shaken in order of precedence. Alphabetical order is out of the question, especially when you consider that the Chinese

127

version is calculated by counting the number of brushstrokes in the surname.

The British Ambassador introduced his illustrious visitor to the Chinese official greeters and to the British military attaché, whose particular job, it was rumoured, was to make sure that the War Leader's Husband didn't run into difficulties with the *mao tai*. A clear white local fluid in which toasts are drunk, *mao tai* has the same effect as inserting your head in a cupboard and asking a large male friend to slam the door.

Every world power, down to and including the Fiji islands, likes to think that its indigenous liquor can rob visiting dignitaries of the ability to reason, but let there be no doubt about *mao tai*. China runs on it. Without it, the Chinese hierarchs would be forced to listen to one another. It was therefore plainly advisable that the War Leader's Husband should be limited to a single crucible of the stuff per banquet, if necessary by military force. The Media, needless to add, were under no such compulsion.

Moving a discreet step behind his all-powerful wife, the Husband was looking ravishing in a silk tie of Ming underglaze blue and a smile of inlaid ivory, but it was the War Leader herself who captured all eyes. Her champagne and rhubarb jersey suit recalled painted silk of the Western Han period, her shoes were dawn carnations plucked at dusk, but it was her facial aspect that must have struck the first thrill of awe into her prospective hosts.

Nothing like that skin had been seen since the Ting potters of Hopei produced the last of their palace-quality high-fired white porcelain with the creamy glaze; her hair had the frozen flow of a Fukien figurine from the early Ch'ing; and her eyes were two turquoise bolts from the Forbidden City's Gate of Divine Prowess, an edifice which, it was clear from her manner, was just a hole in a wall compared to the front door of 10 Downing Street.

The official greeters having been dealt with, the War Leader's party climbed into the waiting limousines and howled off towards town, followed closely by the British Media in a variety of specially arranged transport. The basic Chinese written character for any wheeled vehicle looks like a truck axle viewed from above. I was thinking this while standing there alone. The only Media man to watch the plane land instead of being on it, I was now the only Media man left behind at the airport: a bad augury for my first stint as a foreign correspondent.

By the time I reached town in the back of a Mitsubishi minibus laden with ITN camera boxes, the War Leader had lunched privately and was already due to arrive at the Great Hall of the People in the Square of Heavenly Peace, there to press the flesh with the inscrutable notables of the regime's top rank.

The War Leader's transit through China was competing with a simultaneous visitation by Kim Il Sung of North Korea. Despite respectful articles about Mrs Thatcher in the daily papers (both the English-language *China Daily* and the Chinese-language *Renmin Ribao* carried the official No. 10 handout glossy that makes a Shouchou bronze mirror look relatively unpolished) there was a general feeling that Kim was being given the more effusive welcome, possibly as a tribute to his prose style, by which he has already, single-handed, outdone those Chinese encyclopaedists who codified the classic writings into 36,000 volumes nobody ever read.

But if Kim was hogging the local television time, it could only be said that he was, after all, the leader of a fraternal Socialist country attuned to the way of Lenin and Mao, who have the same embalming fluid flowing through their veins even though they now lie in separate mausoleums. The War Leader was something else, something alien. And yet, somehow, something familiar. Where had the Chinese seen that icy strictness before?

There were only a few thousand people in the Square of Heavenly Peace, which meant that it was effectively deserted, because it can hold half a million spontaneously cheering

enthusiasts on a big day. The armies of eight different Western countries paraded there in 1900 without even touching
the sides. But they did leave a lasting feeling of humiliation,
and when you take into account the fact that it was the
British who actually burned down the Summer Palace in
1860 it will be understood that the Chinese were under no
obligation to go berserk with joy. They hung out a few Red
flags and laid on a Combined Services honour guard of
troops all exactly the same size, like one of those terracotta
armies buried by Qin Shi Huangdi in Shaanxi Province, a
district which was even at that moment being toured by the
heavily publicised Kim.

While the War Leader checked the honour guard for any
deviation in altitude, Peking's only remaining large portrait
of Mao looked down from the Gate of Heavenly Peace across
the thinly populated square. Some Young Pioneers suddenly
slapped their tambourines but the War Leader didn't flinch.
She didn't smile at them either. She was a mask, no doubt
practising her inscrutability for the encounter with Premier
Zhao Ziyang, whom she accompanied inside, there to begin
the opening dialogue which instantly became famous as the
Great Fog Conversation.

Among the gilt friezes and cream plaster columns of the
Great Hall, far below a ceiling full of late-Odeon period light
fittings with frosted globes, Zhao Ziyang, the man whose
name sounds like a ricochet in a canyon, asked the War
Leader whether the cause of fog in London had anything to
do with the climate. His guest said that it was due to the
burning of coal but now there was no coal burned, so there
was no fog. But people in Peking, her host countered, burn
much coal, yet there is no fog. Clearly he had no intention of
letting the point go, but her tenacity equalled his, and as the
Media were ushered from the hall the War Leader was to be
heard giving Zowie a chemistry lesson. Apparently the coal
smoke had been more concentrated in London than it ever
could be in Peking.

The Welcoming Banquet that night was in the Banqueting

Hall of the Great Hall of the People: different room, same light fittings. The War Leader was in a long dress the colour of potassium permanganate, thus to drive home her superiority in chemistry. Zowie's speech was tough on the Hegemonists, meaning the Soviet Union and Israel. Of China's hegemonial activities in Tibet, not a mention. He sat down and she stood up, to deliver a speech ten times as Chinese as his, both in its subtlety and range of cultural reference. She quoted 'one of your T'ang poets' to the effect that distance need be no division. The T'ang poet in question was, I am able to reveal, Wang Wei, but for her to name him would have sounded like showing off.

She was far enough ahead already, since Zowie had neglected to quote even a single Lake poet. There was also the possibility that she was making an arcane reference to Mao, who was, in his own poetry, much drawn to the T'ang style. Out there, hovering above his mausoleum, his immortal spirit was no doubt wondering whether his successors would be up to handling a woman of this calibre. Inside the mausoleum, his wax-filled corporeal manifestation lost one of its ears some time ago but it was rapidly sewn back on, thus restoring the physical integrity which had been denied to his fellow artist Vincent van Gogh. Mao was out of it, but Zowie was in the land of the living, where the real decisions are made.

There were two main toasts, both taken in *mao tai*. The Media watched the War Leader's Husband, and pooled their observations afterwards. The consensus of their data was that he had scored a hole-in-one on the first but had settled for a par four on the second. Behind the flower-and-frond, yellow-dove-decorated centrepiece of the main table, the War Leader and the Premier kept talking. Nobody knew what they had said during the afternoon, but it seemed possible that the War Leader had now shifted the subject of casual conversation from fog to the light fittings. She spent a lot of time looking at them, when not eating. The military orchestra played a rhythmically questionable cha-cha, but the food was sensational, especially a crispy noodle pancake which the Westerners attacked futilely with chopsticks until they noticed the Chinese sensibly picking it up with their fingers.

Next morning, before more talks with the War Leader, Zowie told the assembled Media that there was no prospect of the Chinese yielding on the very point at issue, namely Hong Kong. Since the assembled Media included the Hong Kong Media, there was some consternation at this show of inflexibility, but as far as I know only one foreign correspondent, myself, formed the opinion that it might have been prompted by fear. Even without the Falklands Factor, Mrs Thatcher would have been perceived by the Chinese as a strong woman. Indeed they call her the Strong Woman. But in addition to her already renowned strictness she had fought and won a war. That rings a bell with the Chinese – a large bronze *chung* bell of the Western Chou period, decorated with projecting knobs and interlaced dragons.

The Chinese think historically at all times, and in their long history there have been at least three notoriously tough women: the Empress Wu of the T'ang dynasty, the Empress Dowager Ci Xi of the Chi'ing dynasty, and Jiang Qing of the Mao dynasty, otherwise known as Madame Mao. Though none of these women, especially the last, could be considered precisely sound from the modern Socialist viewpoint, they had undoubtedly shared the virtue of decisiveness.

The Empress Wu, for example, had ascended from the status of Grade Four concubine (massage and hot towels) all the way to the throne, partly through having a child by the Emperor, smothering it, and pointing the finger at his favourite. Having attained unchallenged rule, she dealt with any potential criticism by depriving its perpetrator of all four limbs and keeping what was left alive in a jar of pickle, or hanging it up on a hook.

Mrs Thatcher had not been quite so firm with Norman St John-Stevas, but there could be little doubt that she belonged to a great tradition. She was the Fourth Strong Woman in

Chinese history, an invader from the strange kingdom of the Two Queens, in which one Queen stayed at home minding the palace while the other came marching towards you carrying a severely cut handbag like an Anyang Shang dagger-axe with a jade blade. Give her an inch and she would take the whole of Chang'an Avenue, from the Dongdan intersection to the Babaoshan Cemetery for Revolutionaries (number 10 bus).

After further secret conversations with Zowie about fog and light fittings, the Strong Woman arrived at the British Embassy to meet the British and Chinese communities. This was the second big party of the year for the diplomats of the China station. The first had been the QBP (Queen's Birthday Party), but that was an annual event, well understood. This one was for the other Queen, the one that gets out there and wins wars.

For many of the minor diplomatic faces it was a big moment in a hard life. The Strong Woman gratified them by looking her best, in a plum-blossom and quince-juice silk dress finely calculated to remind Chinese guests of a *mo ku* painting of the Late Northern Sung, although the Chinese might equally have reminded her that William the Conqueror successfully invaded England during that period.

But the garden party was not an occasion for confrontation. Instead she socialised, meeting, *inter alios*, the delightful Katherine Flower, presenter of BBC TV's 'Follow Me', which teaches English to the Chinese. Francis Matthews, the star actor in the programme, is the most famous British face in China. Katherine comes second and Mrs Thatcher third, but by this time she was catching up fast, although getting barely half as much air time as Kim Il Sung, who was still checking out that terracotta army. Perhaps he had at last found the ideal audience for his brand of oratory: statues don't shuffle. Also present at the garden party was the Hong Kong shipping magnate Sir Y. K. Pao. Destined to crop up everywhere in the itinerary, Powie is a name you should note. He and the War Leader go back a long way together, to the time, one gathers, when he was before the mast and she was being called to the bar.

Thursday afternoon was culture gulch, meaning that the Strong Woman could plan her upcoming talks with Deputy Prime Minister Deng Xiaoping while her face and feet were on automatic pilot. At the Conservatory of Music there was much emphasis on Beethoven, of whom there is a plaster bust in even the most humble homes, but the star act was undoubtedly the girl Wu Man. Later on she will be the woman Wu Man, but punning on Chinese names is a low form of humour. Meanwhile she is the best young player of the *pipa* in China. On the *pipa*, which is less unlike a zither than it is unlike anything else, Wu Man played some dance music of the Yi tribe. The Yi tribe sounded like a fun outfit, and for a moment the War Leader relaxed.

Relaxing at the British Book Exhibition was less easy, because the joint was packed with a chosen spontaneous crowd of nervous intellectuals. One of my own books was among the carefully selected thousand and I had visions of helping to make a three-pronged impact on China's spiritual future, along with Margaret Drabble and Iris Murdoch, but there is the problem of distribution. The War Leader's Husband found it hard to see why all the rest of the Chinese couldn't just walk into the library like this lot and sit down to read. A very impressive British Council lady, who speaks effortless Mandarin and is also able to communicate with the Strong Woman's Man, explained that there was a considerable number of Chinese out there, many of them living quite a long way away.

After the standard plum-blossom beauty of a Peking sunset the War Leader dined privately with the British business community while the Media formed groups to eat Peking Duck, a large beast which needs a team of people sitting around its perimeter and all eating inwards for several hours before it disappears. Apart from duck demolition there is practically nothing to do in Peking after 10 p.m. except dance to old Fats Domino 45 rpm EPs, usually on your own. The

Chinese opera on television is OK if you like acrobats. Then comes a blank hissing screen followed by a fitful sleep and one million bicycle bells at dawn. It is Friday, and the population is on the move again.

So was the War Leader, entering the increasingly familiar Great Hall of the People for the first meeting with Deputy Prime Minister Deng Xiaoping, hero of the biggest come-back story since de Gaulle. Mrs Mao had him down and almost out, but he hung in. Deng knows a Strong Woman when he sees one. He was seeing one now, with the straw-berry-blotched blue taffeta suavely off-setting the *cloisonné* enamel of her *maquillage*, so reminiscent of a Ming dynasty incense-burner. He had heard how Zhao had been bested in the Great Fog Conversation, but Zhao was a youngster. He, Deng, was an old hand.

Deng initiated the Great Food Conversation, using the Governor of Hong Kong, invited for that very purpose, as an unwitting foil. Deng said it had been great fun welcoming Kim Il Sung. Having thrown his right, he crossed with his left, saying the food had been very good in Sichuan. The Governor of Hong Kong agreed that the food was good in Sichuan. But the War Leader refused to be drawn. She said that on her earlier visit to China – managing to imply that she would visit China more often if there were not so many wars to win – she had found the food best in Suzhou. 'Well,' said Deng, 'I don't think so.' He had been forced into a hollow protestation, an uncomfortable position for beginning secret talks. The widow of Chou En-lai, holding a bouquet of roses specially flown out by British Airways, complimented the War Leader on her wisdom and tact. 'At your age,' she added, 'it can be said it is the Golden Age.' The Strong Woman took the compliment as her due, forgetting to return it. What was she, a devil? For in the great Sung paint-ing 'The Picture of the Search in the Mountain,' are not the women of angelic appearance more ferocious than the dragons?

The War Leader stumbled on the way down the steps but

the Media's excitement soon subsided – she was merely preoccupied, not fatigued. Off she went with the Chinese for a visit to the Summer Palace, the replacement, on a different site, for the one the British burned down. Actually the interloping forces burned down the replacement too, but it had been replaced again. If the Chinese should bring this awkward subject up, she could always remind them that they, in turn, burned down the British Embassy in the days of the Cultural Revolution.

Later on Friday afternoon the Media were granted access to the War Leader so that she could announce what sounded like a stand-off in negotiations. Confucians among the Media might have said her voice was choked with emotion. T'ang positivists might have said she had Negotiator's Throat. She herself could hardly speak, but this fact meant nothing unless you could see what shape Deng was in, and he wasn't available.

It was a pity that, whether for protocol reasons or because of strained vocal cords, Deng didn't show up at the Return Banquet thrown by the visiting team in the Great Hall of the People, because the War Leader had saved her most stunning outfit until last. A magenta silk gown that recalled Chi'en-lung *flambeau* ware at its most exquisitely uninhibited, it clashed with the pink tasselled chairs, but that wasn't her problem. Let them change the chairs. Her throat was still in tatters but she delivered a Chinese proverb in both languages. 'It is better to come and see for yourself than to read a hundred reports.' The Chinese version sounded a bit short. The Party functionary sitting beside me described it as 'understandable'. His name was Fang so I did not argue.

Zowie's return speech was the usual railway station announcement read at high speed, but when the eating started he indicated bilateral flexibility by employing a fork. The toasting fluid was a pale British equivalent of *mao tai*, and some of the British dishes bore a close resemblance to shark's fin soup and fish lips, but the imported thin mints were a hit. The rapidly improving military band played a very good

arrangement of 'Greensleeves'. There are some instrument-
alists in that combo who would make von Karajan drop his
whip.

As they dined on relentlessly, it was dusk outside, with the
curved yellow-tiled roofs of the Forbidden City glowing softly
like honeycomb through a sea of grey powder. The War
Leader had chosen the right time for Peking – a time of
transition, when the Lotus Lake in the Winter Palace Park is
thick with green leaves, after the blossoms have fallen and
before the roots have been collected to be eaten. Out on the
lake rises the Jade Island, coming to a point, like a lovely
pimple, in the dome of the White Dagoba. When Mrs Mao
was at the height of her power, she closed the Winter Palace
Park to the people and reserved the Jade Island for her own
use, so that she could ride her horse in private.

In China's history, a few women are tyrants and millions
of them are chattels. The problem is to make them something
in between. You can still see thousands of women in Peking
whose feet were bound when they were young. You can't
miss that awkward splay-footed walk: they must forever
struggle to keep their balance. Feet are no longer bound but
that does not mean that minds are free. Despite everything
the Revolution can do, the women still serve the men, the
girls are still snobs who marry boys who get ahead, and you
still can't get ahead without connections. The Revolution,
like any other Chinese dynasty, is behind the times. Margaret Thatcher is a democratic product to an extent of which
even the most radical Chinese theorist can hardly dream.
She doesn't even have to think about it, and often forgets to.

On Saturday morning the Strong Woman rose into the air,
heading for Shanghai with the Media clinging to her wings.
After that would come Canton, with Hong Kong soothingly
employed as the gate of departure. For does not Wang Wei's
poem say that a chip off the dragon's tooth is a spear in its
side? No, it does not. I made that one up.

September 26, 1982

Mrs T. in China

2 The Great Leap Homeward

HER NEGOTIATIONS in Peking for the nonce complete, the
Dragon Lady flew south towards Shanghai, altering her
image in mid-air, as dragons are wont to do. For the purpose
of hard bargaining with the Chinese political leaders she had
been the Woman of Jade, a material so tough that it was not
until the period of the Warring States that the tools were
discovered which could make it fully workable into such
treasurable artefacts as the *pi* disc. But now her purpose was
to spread enlightenment, so she took on the aspect of the
Woman of Science, Yin Sage of the Book of Changes, Adept
of the sixty-four Symbolic Hexagrams, and regular reader of
the *New Scientist*. Corralled into the back end of her winged
conveyance, the British Media, showing distinct signs of
wear, resigned themselves to yet another punishing schedule.

The Yin Sage arrived in Shanghai to find herself lunching
with the omnipresent Hong Kong shipping magnate Sir
Y.K. Pao, a sort of soy-sauce Onassis. The Chinese need
Powie to build ships, but unfortunately for them Powie's
expertise comes accompanied by his personality. Powie puts
on a show of dynamism that makes Jimmy Goldsmith seem
like a Taoist contemplative. As an old pal of the British Prime
Minister, Powie was well placed to make her visit look like an
occasion for which he had helped grease the wheels.

The PM's advisers must have realised that it was enough
for her to be representing democracy without also representing capitalism in one of its more unpalatably flagrant
forms, because the bleary-eyed British Media were eventually allowed to get the impression that Powie's knighthood did
not, in HMG's view, necessarily entitle him to behave as if he

were carrying ambassadorial credentials to the Far East. But
for the moment Powie was at the controls and hustling full
blast. He had a new ship all set to be launched and there were
no prizes for guessing who would swing the bottle.

After the big lunch, the big launch. Shanghai's Jiangnan
shipyards look pretty backward beside the Japanese equivalent, in which half a dozen engineers in snow-white designer
overalls converse with one another by wrist-video while a
team of Kawasaki Unimate robots transforms a heap of raw
materials into a fully computerised bulk carrier with a
jacuzzi in the captain's bathroom. Here there were about a
thousand Chinese queueing up to borrow the spanner. But
the atmosphere was festive. An air of spontaneity – real
spontaneity, as opposed to the mechanical variety laid on by
Party directives – was generated by a band truck tricked out
with balloons and dispensing the Shanghai equivalent of
Chicago jazz. A very big drum and several different sizes of
gong combined to produce the typical Chinese orchestral
texture of many obsolete fire-alarms going off at once.

Next to the completed ship, which Powie had cunningly
named *World Goodwill*, there was a sign in English saying BE
CAREFUL NOT TO DROP INTO THE RIVER. The Yin Sage was
dressed in navy blue with a white hat, thereby establishing a
nautical nuance, an impression furthered by her consort's
azure tie. Actually it was the same tie he had worn when
arriving in Peking, but this was a different city, and in China
every city is a whole new nation. It is not just that there are a
thousand million Chinese who have never seen the world.
There are a thousand million Chinese who have never seen
China. So if you wear the same tie at different ends of the
country it is unlikely that you will cause the locals to whisper
behind their hands. No stranger to the Far East, the Yin
Sage's Yang Companion has got such considerations well
taped.

Powie rose to his Gucci-shod feet in order to convince
anybody who still needed convincing that he bears a truly
remarkable resemblance to the late Edward G. Robinson. He

thanked his distinguished sponsor for being there. He thanked everybody else for being there as well. He thanked the Chinese Government for its breadth of vision. He was on the point of thanking the population of China individually, but the Woman of Science had a schedule to meet. Referring, in her Falklandish capacity as a connoisseur of naval architecture, to 'this splendid ship', she spoke of how it epitomised the ability of Socialist China and the freely enterprising West to work in harmony. 'This ship . . . is a symbol of the close relationship.' It was a relationship ship.

She launched the relationship ship by swinging an axe to cut the line that released the bottle. The bottle declined to break, but according to Chinese tradition it is the blow of the axe which matters, not the result. In the *I Ching*, according to the great naturalist philosopher Chu Hsi's justly celebrated interpretation, *Li*, the cosmic principle of organisation at all levels, is coterminous with and ultimately inseparable from *chhi*, or matter-energy. To put it another way, it's the thought that counts.

The relationship ship was already in the water and thus destined to remain immobile after being launched, but the band truck, or Truck of Good Luck, erupted into a rousing rendition of its signature tune, 'Seven Ancient Fire-Engines Failing to Discover the Location of Chow Fong's Burning House'. The Yin Sage, charmingly referred to by a nervous young female interpreter as 'the Rather Honourable Margaret Thatcher', took leave of Powie with the air of one who knows that the separation will be all too short.

She was headed for the Shanghai Institute of Biochemistry of the Academica Sinica, whither all the British Media, except one, decided not to accompany her. My colleagues, wise in the trade, had knowledgeably concluded that now was the time to file their copy, take a well-earned nap, or check out the attractions of what had once been China's most westernised big city, the first one to import every occidental fad up to and including Communism. In Shanghai it is even possible to buy an alcoholic drink if you turn the right corners. The girls are just as unattainable as in Peking but they dress more provocatively, with a cut to their comradely trousers which suggests that they are not above withholding some of their labour from the commune in order to sit up at night resewing the odd seam.

It would have been good to spend more than just a few minutes following Sidney Greenstreet's ghost past the old Western Concession compounds of the Bund, and on top of that there was the Shanghai National Museum, containing pictures which I had been waiting to see half my life, and of which I can only say that if I could write the way those guys painted I would use up a lot less Tipp-Ex. But like a fool I went to the Biochemistry Institute, and like a fool I got lucky. The Woman of Science put on her best public performance of the tour so far, and I was the only scribe there to cover it.

The performance was good because for once she wasn't performing. Biochemistry is her field and the assembled scientists were among the top boys in it, so when they spoke she was for a moment distracted from her usual self-imposed task of proving her superiority to everyone else. The head of the Institute apologised, in beautifully eloquent English, for his English, which he had not spoken for forty years. 'Today we are very honoured to have you with us. First of all, may I introduce Professor . . . ' He introduced a dozen professors, respectively in charge of such departments as insulin synthesis, nucleic acids, biomemory, molecular radiation and a lot of other things I couldn't catch. Most of it was Chinese to me but clearly it was grist to the mill of the Woman of Science, especially the stuff about insulin, which she was concerned with when studying under her famous mentor, the Nobel Prizewinner Dorothy Hodgkin – a name revered by the Shanghai scientists, who had a picture of her in their visitors' book.

That the Yin Sage was Dorothy Hodgkin's Pupil plainly went down a storm with the Chinese, in whom the dynastic principle is well ingrained. The Pupil's pupils sharpened, I noticed, when one of the scientists announced that the laboratory was working on leukaemia and liver cancer. Since the same laboratory had already developed, among other things, such eminently applicable ideas as the reprogramming of fish to breed in still water, there was no need to think they would not crack the case, always provided that their government gave curing old humans the same priority as feeding new ones. Of these latter, needless to say, there is no shortage, and in fact the Shanghai laboratory is working on a fertility drug (derived from the same LH–RH analysis that fixed the fish) which could produce irreversible infertility at high dosages – a possibility which the Woman of Science immediately saw might be open to abuse, and said so.

Touring the individual laboratories, she interviewed the scientists working in each. They all spoke dazzling scientific English, with words like 'cucumber' falsely emphasised and phrases like 'polypeptide macromolecular electrokinesis' fluently delivered. After she left each room I backtracked to ask the interviewees, relaxing after their ordeal, whether she still knew her stuff. Without exception they said she did. She missed a trick, though, in the room where they analyse proteins by counting dots. Reminiscing, the Woman of Science said: 'We had no computers in those days to analyse the dots.' Her hosts were too polite to tell her the truth, which was that as far as they were concerned those days were still here. Even to the inexpert eye, the laboratory is painfully underequipped. The rubber tubes are perished, glass is hoarded like gold, and there is obviously no more computer time in a year than there are rainy days in the Gobi. They're counting those dots with an abacus. When the Woman of Science handed a Sinclair desk computer to the Japanese it was coals to Newcastle, or at any rate bamboo shoots to Tokyo. The same computer given to the Shanghai Biochemistry Institute would have made some long friends.

The banquet that night was hosted by the Mayor of Shanghai, who generously announced in his speech of welcome that 'British people have always had a great feeling for the Chinese'. He could have put this another way, saying

that British people were instrumental in poisoning half the
country with opium and showed an enthusiasm unusual
even among the European nations when it came to humili-
ating the Chinese by such practices as shutting them out of
their own cities. The park which was denied to 'dogs and
Chinese' is still there on the river side of the Bund. Nowadays
it is enjoyed by the indigenous population but they allow us
to share it, which is a lot more than we ever did for them. One
only hoped that the Yin Sage knew how tactful the Mayor
was being in not mentioning any of that.

The possibility that the Woman of Science might be a bit
thin in the area of Chinese history was a constant worry to
those of us in her entourage who wished her well on her
delicate mission. But she caught all eyes in her dress of vivid
K'ang-hsi cobalt blue, a veiled reminder that in the eighteenth
century (our time) the European demand for Chinese porcelain was matched by an equally eager supply. The Mayor,
perhaps forewarned, had countered in advance by gracing
every table with a full kit of Yi Sing stoneware specially
procured for the occasion. It looked like bitter chocolate and
provided an ideal container for the dreaded *mao tai*, the liquid
land-mine, the anti-personnel potion employed by Chinese
functionaries to render one another's official speeches in-
audible. Since first encountering the stuff a week before, the
British Media had settled on two ways of coping with it. You
could down it in one and get drunk straight away or you
could sip at it and get drunk almost straight away.

In Shanghai, however, one was likely to forget about
drinking in favour of eating, because the food was astonishing – compared with Peking, there was a playful savour to its
presentation which suggested that we were already getting
closer to the West. The same thing was suggested by the
attire and general demeanour of the waitresses, who wore
skirts instead of trousers and in an alarming number of cases
were unmanningly pretty. British scriveners and cameramen
fought one another for a smile. If you are the kind of man who
falls in love through the eyes, you will fall in love a hundred

times a day in China. No wonder that in the Chinese artistic heritage the pictures outweigh the words and even the words are pictures. The whole place soaks the optic nerve like a long shot of morphine into a fresh vein. I smiled like a goof from daylight to dusk.

Among those prominent behind the top table's array of carved pumpkins was the inevitable Powie. The Mayor referred to him as 'Mr' Y.K. Pao, thereby depriving him of his knighthood, which he must have received for services to athletics, because when the Woman of Science went up to congratulate the orchestra Powie was out of his starting blocks and congratulating them right along with her. The great Australian sprinter Hector Hogan used to move that fast but he needed spiked shoes to do it.

Onward to Canton, where there was another banquet, this time for lunch instead of dinner. The venue was the Dongfang hotel, a Disneyland Chinese emporium all dolled up in funfair gilt filigree. By now you could feel the West close by, just outside the Pearl River delta, a jetfoil ride across a short stretch of the South China Sea. People from Hong Kong come here to visit their relatives and give them that greatest of all gifts, a television set. The girls at the cashier's desk have pocket calculators which the scientists in Shanghai would covet and which the clerks in the Minzu hotel in Peking would probably fail to recognise. China is a big place. Here, at the edge, it is a bit like the West, but the edge, we had learned, is a long way from the middle.

We were all Old China Hands now. Even the Woman of Science, clad today in a green dress recalling the *famille verte* teapots of the Ch'ing, was looking blasé. The locals kept bringing forth food fit to change the mind of anyone who had been harbouring the notion that Cantonese cuisine means offal rolled in red ochre and glazed like a brick. It was wonderful, but after a week of banqueting we had had enough. The Yin Sage's impeccable chopstick technique did not falter. She could still pick up a greased peanut without lifting either elbow. But her usually transparent azure eyes had grown slightly occluded, like the milky-violet glaze which the Chinese collectors of ceramics call *kuei-mien-ch'ing*, or ghost's-face blue. Perhaps she had seen too much of Powie.

She escaped him on the short flight to Hong Kong. When her plane took off he was not on it. I was not on it either, having failed to fill out the right forms some weeks before. After several hours spent anxiously facing the prospect of staying in China for ever – imagine how long it will be before they get breakfast television – I secured the last seat on a packed Trident and scrambled aboard. As I came stooping through the door I recognised a certain pair of Gucci shoes. It was Powie. He assured me that Mrs Thatcher's trip was 'very successful' and that she had done a grand job. Powie has a lot in common with David Frost – permanent jet-lag, an unusual way with the English language, and an infallible nose for the main action.

The approach to Kai Tak, Hong Kong's notorious airport, starts between mountains and continues between buildings. As the joke says, Hong Kong is the only city where street-vendors sell you things before you land. The place struck me, even at the very moment when I thought I was about to strike it, as a kind of slant-eyed Las Vegas. No sooner had the plane stopped rolling than Powie was outside and into a black Toyota, while your reporter was making his solitary and sweat-soaked way to the Hilton, where the rest of the British Media were already up to their necks in pine-scented suds while they filed copy on the bathroom telephone. The wealth of Hong Kong would seem ridiculous anyway, but after the Chinese People's Republic you feel like a nun dropped into Babylon. To dial room service is to experience disgust, and for half an hour I hesitated. All right, half a minute.

The Dragon Lady, guarded by police SWAT squads up on the roofs, had by now transformed herself into the Keeper of Secrets. The fate of Hong Kong, known to her faithful consort as Honkers, was locked in her mind and safe from divination, even by the methods of geomancy or *feng-shui* (the winds and the waters). While the Hong Kong Media went

crazy with speculation, she did her chores, starting with a
visit to the Scots Guards at Stanley Fort. After Northern
Ireland, Honkers is a cushy posting. The wives swim in the
clear water of Repulse Bay and have babies while the going is
good. The Keeper of Secrets dropped out of the sky by
helicopter and moved among them in a midnight-blue dress
sprinkled with almond blossoms. The heat was breathtaking.
'Are you *all* pregnant?' she asked. The teeth of a pretty
child called Joanna were duly inspected. The British Media
rushed to interview Joanna. I interviewed the wives, who all
said, without being prompted, that their visitor looked too
tired to last out the day.

As she climbed back into the thwacking helicopter, one
could only agree. Her stamina is impressive but she is overly
proud of it, and this trip she had pushed herself too far. Along
with the punch-drunk British Media I strapped myself into
the back-up helicopter and found myself hanging into space
over an open door with Kowloon lying sideways underneath.
If she felt half as bad as I did then the upcoming, all-
important press conference was going to be a disaster.

In fact, it was her best yet. On the last day in Peking she
had made a bad press conference worse by showing obvious
impatience with the halting English of some of the Hong
Kong Media. This propensity probably springs less from
intolerance than from her urge to get cracking, but to possess
it is a handicap and to indulge it is a grievous fault. Now,
however, on the day that mattered, she kept her irascibility
bottled up. She said all she could say, which was that an
agreement had been reached that there should be an agreement, and that from here on in it was all down to the
diplomats. When a Hong Kong girl reporter said that the
question of renewing the lease could have simply been
ignored, the Stateswoman turned a potential minus into a
plus by insisting that a contract is a contract and the means of
meeting it should be found early, 'in good time'. Clearly she
spoke with conviction, from the deep core of her nature,
where the Good Housekeeping Seal of Approval has the force

of law. In Peking she had got away for a few minutes on her own in search of a bolt of fabric. The one she liked was too pricey at £39 a yard, so she had not bought it. Her passion for managing the household along sound lines was what got her elected in the first place, and was what now reassured the people of Hong Kong that things might just conceivably, in the long run, be going to be all right. On Hong Kong television the assembled pundits, posing in front of blown-up Thatcher glossies that looked like publicity stills of Eleanor Parker in *Return to Peyton Place*, began a long analysis of what little she had said, as if there could have been more. Next day the stock market dipped but there was no crash. When the rabbits had finished pulling out, the smart money would probably buy back in.

The smart money was there in force at the Government House reception. Chinese businessmen whose personal wealth made Powie look like a pauper were jostling to breathe the Dragon Lady's perfume. If her mission had been a flop then they would already have been in Acapulco, so the signs were favourable. I met such mighty Hong Kong *tai pan*s as Mr Lee of real estate, Mr Fong of many boats, and the ineffable Sir Run Run Shaw, who had made a hill of money out of those terrible films in which bad actors kick each other. (In the days when he was plain Mister, Run Run invented a cinematic process called Shawscope, a version of the wide-screen ratio which allowed more actors to kick each other at the same time.) One after the other I asked all these characters whether they had been in Peking lately. It turned out that all of them had been spending a lot of time there. Mr Lee told me how much the Chinese leaders respected his honesty.

So the boys are smoothing the road to the inevitable. Only Sir Run Run had the cheek to say that if a new regime asked him to make a Socialist movie he would run-run for cover. Actually it is hard to see why he should be worried: his movies would be readily adaptable to Marxist–Leninist ideological content. Just make the bad guys the capitalists and the good guys could start kicking again straight away.

The Dragon Lady's VC-10 screamed out of Kai Tak like a fighter and banked steeply towards India. All RAF transport aircraft have the passenger seats facing backwards, so the British Media, once again confined to the rear of the aircraft, could see where they had been. Laden down with electronic devices and paper kites for the children, they were too tired to sleep. So was the Dragon Lady, but she had no choice. Soon it would be the Conservative Party Conference. It was time for another transformation. The cabin lights went out to denote that she had retired. Her mind stirred in the darkness, putting away China and putting on Britain, forgetting Zhao Ziang and remembering Francis Pym. She was turning herself back into a Party Leader. While she dreamed and the Media drank, I looked back through the window along the Road of Silk, the ancient trade route which brought Marco Polo to Cathay and the Land of Prester John, and which was already old when Chinese lacquer boxes were on sale in the markets of Imperial Rome.

As you might have gathered, I loved China. But Westerners have always loved China. In the last century they drugged her, stripped her naked, tied her hands above her head, and loved her as they pleased. We were lucky that a revolution was all that happened. If we are luckier still, the current bunch of Chinese gerontocrats will be smoothly replaced by a generation of intellectuals who were so appalled at the Cultural Revolution that they are now less frightened by democracy than by despotism. If that happens, the Chinese revolution might manage what the Soviet version so obviously can't – to civilise itself. Here, as in every other aspect of Chinese life, tradition is a comfort. China knew totalitarianism two hundred years before Christ, when the mad First Emperor of the Ch'in obliterated all memory of the ancient glory of Chou, burned the classical texts and put to death anybody caught reading the *Book of Songs*. But he unified the tribes, and on that strong base rose the majestic dynasty of Han, on whose era the Chinese of today still pride themselves, as will the Chinese of tomorrow.

In Delhi Mrs Thatcher had breakfast with Mrs Gandhi: a hen session. In Bahrain she shook hands with a sheik. At 34,000 feet over Europe she invited the Media forward for a drink. God knows what she thought of us: prominent in the front row of the scrum were at least two journalists who had been blotto since Peking. As for what we thought of her, the answer is not easy. Some had their prejudices confirmed. None thought less of her. I still wouldn't vote for her, because I favour the Third Way, the Way of Tao, in which the universal principle is made manifest through the interlocking forms of David Steel and Roy Jenkins.

But I had grown to admire her. She is what she is, and not another thing, and on such issues it is better to be crassly straight than subtly devious. Perhaps being haunted by the Falklands, where for want of a nail she was obliged to send many young men to their deaths, in the matter of Hong Kong she seemed determined to be well prepared. The business touches me personally, because on Hong Kong Island, in the war cemetery at Sai Wan Bay, my father has lain since 1945, cut down at the age of thirty-three because the British did not know how to avoid a war in the Pacific. If firm talk and a steely glance can stop that happening again, Mrs Thatcher is ideal casting. She deserves credit for her iron guts, even if you think her brains are made of the same stuff.

While thinking all this I was searching the cabin. He wasn't there. Finally I wangled an invitation to the flight deck. He wasn't there either. Powie was not at the controls. She had got away from him at last. As the VC-10 dived towards Heathrow the wings suddenly shone like water gardens. After ten days and a dozen countries it was raining for the first time. The Han dragons could control the rain but ours must have been too tired. She had just enough energy for the last transformation, into the mother of her children. Mr and Mrs Thatcher stepped down to embrace their son Mark, who had driven all the way from town without getting lost once.

October 3, 1982

Postcard from Epcot

A TECHNOLOGICAL fun-fair made possible by the micro-processor and mankind's allegedly unflagging respon-siveness to the cuddly warmth of Mickey Mouse, Epcot is the Walt Disney organisation's latest and most awe-inspiring addition to the large part of central Florida known as the Vacation Kingdom. From the moment I first heard about Epcot I knew I would do almost anything to get out of going there, but duty called.

Epcot sounds like an anagram but isn't, unless Cotpe and Pocet are scatological words in the language of the Aztecs. Mexico is just around the gulf from Florida so perhaps that's the connection. I was thinking this while reading the Epcot brochure on the way across the Atlantic by British Cale-donian DC-10. The prose helped set the mood. 'Epcot Center represents the ultimate in Disney-Imagineered enter-tainment . . . a celebration of ingenuity and innovation . . . the incredible visions of Walt Disney . . . the Epcot Experi-ence.'

If the late Walt Disney's visionary capacity had indeed remained operational beyond the tomb, then the word 'in-credible' seemed hardly sufficient to fit the case, but that was a quibble. The British Caledonian Experience included some reassuringly larky hostesses in plaid skirts. Had they been heading straight back to Gatwick, instead of stopping over in Atlanta, I would probably have begged to go with them.

Atlanta airport gives you your first taste of the Epcot Experience. A computerised mini-train with a flat voice takes you to the passenger processing centre. 'This is Concourse A. The next stop is Concourse B. The colour-coded maps and signs in the vehicle match the colours in the Concourse.' The paging system has a real human voice calling out real human names ('Would Gloria Raspberry, Slope Middleton and John Lurching please go to a white pay phone and dial zero for a message?'), but in all other respects the machines are in control, running a complex whose sheer size reminds you that the South is the new wealth centre of the USA.

After a quick Eastern Airlines interstate flight to Orlando in Florida, you get an even stronger reminder. Eastern is billed as the Official Walt Disney World Airline and Orlando's airport is just as thoroughly automated as Atlanta's. Thanks to the Vacation Kingdom, tourism is the Number One industry in the area, with the traditional citrus and cattle running second and third. But coming up fast in fourth place is technology. Just as Florida's Walt Disney Magic Kingdom copies the Californian Disneyland but gives itself more room, so the Florida equivalent of Silicon Valley turns out the same chips but at a lower overhead. With Kennedy Space Center only an hour down the tollway, not even the sky is the limit.

The Mickey Mouse touch-telephones in my hotel room were a token of how Epcot marries advanced electronics to the hallowed Disney ideal of anthropomorphised model animals who insist on being your friend. A special television channel with a Slim Pickens-type Southern Fried voice-over described Epcart as a noo world of wonder and a leading Florida traction – traction being the opposite of repulsion. So I was already well prepared for Epcot's initial impact by the time I became a statistic at the turnstile.

The turnstiles are overshadowed by the eighteen-storey geodesic globe housing Spaceship Earth, a ride sponsored by the Bell System. Bell's big ball stands for both main themes of Epcot: Future World, which is composed of the high-tech display structures contributed by the respective industrial sponsors, and World Showcase, a series of lakeshore pavilions non-controversially encapsulating the way of life in various countries. The big ball, in short, symbolises the international cultural unity which must inevitably accrue as our planet, singing in harmony like the Mickey Mouse Club choir, spins confidently into the future.

The big ball also symbolises another of Epcot's recurring themes, the balls-up. On my first day's visit Spaceship Earth had conked out and didn't get started until after nightfall, by which time the intestinally convoluted queue of waiting customers would, if straightened out, have stretched to the Magic Kingdom, two-and-a-half miles away by monorail. So I left that one for later and queued up for the Universe of Energy, sponsored by Exxon. Many of the people in the queue were very fat, so that if you wanted to see what was happening at the turnstile you had to take a few steps to one side. Epcot is indeed tracting 'guests' from all over the world, but most of the guests it tracts are Americans; of those, most are Southerners; and of those, an impressive proportion are of enormous girth, a fact emphasised by their special vacation clothes.

As one who must watch his weight lest it double overnight, I was chastened to be in the presence of a whole population whose idea of weight-watching is to watch other people's weight while adding to their own. Imperfectly circular men and women clad in T-shirts and running shorts snacked their way through one-pound bags of peanut brittle. They all wore training shoes. Training for what? A heart attack? That the rides should keep breaking down no longer seemed quite such a mystery.

Inside the pavilion there was a hundred-piece multi-screen movie plus stereo song. 'Ener-gee! Bringing our world new graces!' Then we went through into an environment of rhubarb lurex drapes with blocks of seats looking like cut-down buses minus wheels. 'You are seated in an Epcot innovation, the Travelling Theater,' said a tape proudly. 'Keep your hands and arms inside the vehicle at all times.' Another wrap-around movie told us about energy in the past. Then the screen rolled up and we rumbled forward to see what the past looked like.

'Come with us', boomed a doomy tape, 'into the Mesozoic age.' 'Where we *goin*'?' asked the large lady filling the row of

seats beside me. 'Oh my! Whoo-*ee*! Lookit *that*!' The Mesozoic turned out to be a block-long diorama with dinosaurs
looming out of dry-ice fumes. Chips and solenoids gave the
embattled beasts a more subtle repertoire of movement than
the standard Disneyland animated dummies with which we
have long been familiar. Instead of moving their heads from
side to side and their arms up and down, they moved their
heads up and down as well as from side to side, while moving
their arms from side to side as well as up and down. More
interesting was that the all-powerful Epcot master computer
had failed to close the automatic doors in my section of the
Travelling Theater, so there was a chance that if my companion breathed out suddenly I might be propelled into the
Mesozoic, there to be engulfed by primeval steam.

On through the hologram-haunted and diode-decorated
darkness grumbled the solar-powered, computer-guided
Travelling Theater, with the sound system thundering a
continuous testament to 'the genius of the human mind'. But
as the Travelling Theater headed out of the prehistoric
jungle and back into the era of the rhubarb lurex drapes,
suddenly the whole show ground to a halt. '*Mmwah mmwah!*'
said the Travelling Theater, going nowhere. 'Please remain
seated,' said a human voice. 'We are experiencing operating
difficulties.'

The tape moved on to its next cue, which was now out of
sequence with events. 'Welcome back, folks! We hope . . .
click.' The computer must have forgotten to tell the cassette-
player to hit the pause key. An Imagineer appeared out of the
mist, lifted up a panel in the Travelling Theater, and doctor-
ed the hardware. '*Mmwah!*' Still no action. 'We are unable',
said the human voice, 'to continue with our presentation.'
The brochure told us what we had missed. 'The forces of
energy and the part they play in our lives is powerfully
depicted in the show's final act.' It sounded good.

Resolving to give the powerful depiction another chance
later, I tried the World of Motion, sponsored by General
Motors. This one looked like another airline terminal but

the ride was fun, even after you had finished being told how much fun it was going to be. 'When it comes to trans-por*tay*-shun,' sang the hidden stereo, 'it's always *fun* to be FREE.' From GM's viewpoint, you couldn't help suspecting, it would be even more fun to be free from Japanese competition, but be that as it may, the dioramas were witty, with caveman automotive engineers inventing triangular wheels, etc.

There was a bit less than usual of Mickey Mouse's deadly optimism. I always preferred Donald Duck, and even him I could stand only when he was in an evil mood. His nephews were good value, especially when they were setting booby-traps for the Beagle Boys or jockeying fanatically for promotion in the Junior Woodchucks, an organisation which combined all the most pious elements of the Boy Scouts, Rotary and, dare one say it, the Mickey Mouse Club. You felt that in some neglected department of the Walt Disney empire the genius of the human mind was being allowed a measure of scepticism.

So it was here, when the open vehicle in which several colossal ladies and I were bumping through the darkness was abruptly transformed into a hologram of the Automobile of Tomorrow. There was a bubble of light around us through which we all stuck our hands, and in the mirrored walls of the tunnel we could see ourselves travelling in a teardrop. It was an enchanting moment which not even the portentously intoning tape could spoil. 'What challenges await us on the road to the future?' it asked. '*Mmwah!*' replied the vehicle. 'Attention in the world of Motion,' said an amplified voice. 'The ride has temporarily come to a halt and could re-zoom at any moment.'

Journey Into Imagination, sponsored by Kodak, was closed for most of the morning because of an open-air Dedication Ceremony. Hundreds of Walt Disney and Kodak dignitaries sat in a roped-off area while the rest of us rubber-necked across the water terraces and ornamental ponds. 'Imagi*nay*-shern!' bellowed an amplified kick-line of dancing

154

singers in white cat-suits. The President of Walt Disney Productions welcomed Kodak. 'In 1966 I was a rookie for the L.A. Rams. My father-in-law Walt Disney said . . .' The Kodak senior executive rose to reply. 'It's great to be here. And I would also like to say how great it is to have the Kodak All-American football team here with us . . . all of you who share in that dream.'

Sharing in that dream helped offset the awkward fact that Journey Into Imagination's actual journey, heralded as being more complicated than all the other Epcot rides put together, still hasn't been made to work, despite the full-time efforts of an army of Imagineers. But the 3-D movie in the same pavilion does something to compensate for the continuing no-ride mode. Wearing special glasses to watch a squad of differently coloured nauseating children pointing their toys at you might not sound promising, but the results are truly sensational. You reach out to touch things that aren't there.

Lunch in the World Showcase entailed a mad sprint to Italy. People who can't get into Italy turn and leg it towards France, further round the lake. Thus it is revealed why the fat ladies wear running shorts. A scaled-down and cleaned-up Piazza San Marco, Italy is the most popular eating place because of the presence of Alfredo's. Photographs on the wall show the original Alfredo, long ago in the other Italy, stuffing handfuls of spaghetti into Tyrone Power. The Epcot Italy Alfredo's is run by the maestro's grandson and everybody rates the *fettuccine* as a Gormay Meal. But my plateful was like flex melted by an electrical fire and doused with cheese foam. The helping was big enough to choke a shark, as indeed were the helpings of everything else, thus to cater for local expectations. The Gormay Meal and the gargantuan plateful aren't two things you can have at the same time, but most Americans don't know that. The real Alfredo, who did know it, is no doubt spinning in his grave, but his grave is somewhere back there in the alternative Italy and nobody can hear his rattling casket.

Spaceship Earth was still on the blink so I took the mono-rail down to the Magic Kingdom, where Tomorrowland, though now outpaced by Epcot's Future World, would, one assumed, at least offer a reliable ride. The monorail tape proclaimed the virtues of 'always being in a state of becoming', but Tomorrowland seemed to be largely in a state of becoming old hat. Mission to Mars had multi-screens and vibrating plastic seats but where were the lasers and the holograms? Space Mountain, a famously vertiginous roller-coaster whose twin brother I had ridden in the California Disneyland, was at a standstill. 'Attention, space travellers. All space flights have been put in a holding pattern. All travellers in space rockets please remain seated.' Some of the space travellers stuck on the curves looked too heavy to remain seated without the aid of centrifugal force.

Back went the monorail across the dusk-shrouded boondocks to Epcot, now a city of candy-coloured lights with the big ball shining pale blue. Spaceship Earth was at last functioning. The facility was go. Into the car and upward we cranked into the whispering darkness, I alone in the front seat and a married couple the size of the Kodak All-American football team crammed into the back. Holograms of cave-dwellers showed Man discovering his Genius. 'Who are *squawk*?' asked the tape in my headrest. 'Where *squawk* we come from?' '*Squawk* are we going?' A marionette representing Leonardo underwent the Renaissance Experience. Up in the roof of the dome there was a very convincing illusion of being in outer space. The car turned around and went backwards down into the laser-lacerated and diode-dotted Future. We were lying on our backs with the sound coming in at each ear. 'Tomorrow's world approaches. Let us explore and question and understand. Let us *squawk*. *Squawk* us *squawk squawk*.'

After a night spent dreaming about a talking plateful of acrylic *fettuccine* I was back out at Epcot again, all set to give Spaceship Earth another try. 'Having relived our past and eyed our future,' said the brochure, 'we time-passengers are now ready to become captains, to chart our Earth's course toward tomorrow and determine our own destinies.' The tape was probably meant to deliver the same message, but once again the all-wise central computer was either failing to monitor the interference or else was actually causing it.

I heard something of how 'glorious Rome' had been 'consoomed by the flames of *excess*' and of how the Renaissance had been 'a beacon through the mists of time', but after the turnaround in the starry roof – a manoeuvre aided, I now noticed, by a real live Imagineer crouching in the darkness – it was all downhill in every sense. 'We have changed ourselves . . . changed our world . . . from the edge of space to the depths of the sea . . . we have *squawk* ourselves together with an electronic *squawk*.'

The Land, courtesy of Kraft, is a superficially less glamorous but ultimately more satisfying adventure, if only because the little boat you ride in is graced with the presence of a living guide. 'Hi! I'm Thad and I'm gonna take you on a cruise through the Land with which we have a partnership. Let's listen to it. Let's listen to the Land.' *Brrt. Brrt.* Taped insects sent messages of fertility. There weren't just sounds, there were odours and hot winds. Mechanical chickens smelled real. It was Disneyland with chips, but the second half of the ride took you through real crops being grown by noo methods, such as a sky-hook conveyor belt which enables the roots of the plant to be sprayed with water in mid-air. Giant melons and squashes were greeted with approval by the giant people in the boats. 'Lookit them *squorshes*! *So* big. Biggee biggee! Oh *mah*! Whoo-*ee*!'

I lunched quite well in the United Kingdom, at a pub called the Rose and Crown. Authentic except for its cleanliness, the UK was staffed by genuine young Britons, of whom about half were over there on J-1 visas as part of a World Showcase Fellowship Program embracing countless different Learning Experiences, including Future Studies. As with the other participating countries, the UK Fellowship-holders tend to be rather upmarket. A nice young man from a public school gave his present address as Seven Dwarfs Lane, Snow White Campgrounds. He could see the joke but thought that the Learning Experiences would help him in his business studies upon returning home.

It looked like hard work just replacing the merchandise on the shelves. The Americans can't get enough of it. English hand-painted metal chess-sets at $4,000 a box are selling like cookies – no empty phrase when you see how the cookies are selling. Those guests eat *all the time*. In France the queue at the *boulangerie* looked like the early stages of a marathon for Sumo wrestlers.

China hasn't yet opened a restaurant but features a marvellous 360-degree movie, although you might wonder why Tibet gets such a fleeting mention. Only one of the Chinese girls, De Zhen, is actually from China. The others are from Hong Kong and Taiwan. You can't imagine old Deng letting too many of his people out to study 'the Art and Management of the Disney Experience'. Germany has a beer cellar with Hans Sachs-type waiters in Lederhosen. There is no marionette of Hitler but you can't have everything. Indeed as far as politics are concerned you can't have anything. The blandness is total.

Back among the Future World pavilions, I entered Communicore for my final encounter with tomorrow, the Astuter Computer Revue. ('Astuter' is pronounced 'astooter' but 'computer' is pronounced 'computer', according to some linguistic rule beyond my competence.) A hologram extravaganza, the phantom show is projected on to the actual brain centre of Epcot, a Sperry Univac number-cruncher which fills a glassed-in area the size of a Space Center firing-room.

While the computer's human attendants search the software to uncover why the Universe of Energy's Travelling Theater keeps crapping out, a hundred guests at a time look through a glass wall and think they see the machine all lit up with polychromatic laser-trace lattices. The star of the show, for unfathomable reasons, is a sub-Tommy Steele gold-suited cockney entertainer appearing in a miniaturised hologram form that does nothing to make his accent or vocabulary more credible. Dancing eerily among the machine's cabinets, he sings a hymn to its astootness. 'That's why I'm a rooter/For me computer.' The groundlings are open-mouthed, which makes it easier for them to put in the peanut brittle, but only a churl would not be open-mouthed along with them. The ingenuity really is impressive. Nor is there any reason to crow about things going wrong. A constant, public reminder of technology's fallibility is probably just what the real world needs.

What the Walt Disney World needs is a sense of humour, which can't be had without facing facts. Despite Epcot's much-vaunted educational value, it teaches very little worth learning, because it empties the significance from any subject before beginning to expound it. The World Showcase is not a model of tomorrow's harmonious international society. It is a model of nothing except itself. Real countries aren't like that. They have conflicts of interest within themselves and between each other, and always will have. The most they can hope for is to resolve their differences. The message that they should choose peace is not a message. It is empty talk.

So is the message that we can choose our future. The choice is not up to us – not because there is no choice but because there is no us. In its confident assumption that there can be such a thing as a collective will, the Walt Disney World provides democracy's version of totalitarianism – miniaturised instead of monolithic, kindly instead of cruel, but equally drained of all nuance. For real laughter to happen, reality must break through. Most of the laughter I have ever heard in the various branches of the Walt Disney World has been hollow, even from the children. A vast organisation which tells you how to have fun is not the same as an individual being funny.

Walt Disney was funny. If you didn't think him that, at least you couldn't deny that he was creative. Critics who said that his creations were in bad taste missed the point. Genius is often in bad taste. They should have said that he was, at his frequent worst, tasteless – in the sense that a Gormay Meal is all presentation but tastes of nothing. ('A generous portion of tender minute-sized shrimp,' said the menu from which I chose my last Gormay Meal in the Vacation Kingdom, 'doing the backstroke on a sea of lettuce, lemon crown, tomato, olives and egg quarters.') But at least Disney's creatures, no matter how excruciatingly adorable, were to some extent the expression of a single human mind.

On the DC-10 from Atlanta back to London they were showing *Star Wars*. Having seen it too many times, I left my earphones off, but every few minutes my eyelids rolled open and there they were – R2-D2 and C-3PO, the new Mickey and the new Goofy. The future, to the limited extent in which it can be foreseen, belongs to Darth Vader, the Muppets and ET. Porky the Pig doesn't make it into space. Miss Piggy does, on the starship Swine Trek. The computer-generated graphics of the Walt Disney production *TRON* can do little to redress the balance. Trumped by alien creatures, the Walt Disney World has been left characterless.

It had to happen. When the genius of Walt Disney's human mind winked out, it left only his philosophy, which was never anything except business enterprise dressed up with rhetoric. You should see Epcot if you are ever in the Vacation Kingdom, but the best reason for ever being in the Vacation Kingdom is Sea World, whose dolphins and whales remind you that man's creative genius is by no means the greatest thing in creation. The Walt Disney World without Walt Disney is a vision without imagination – the very quality it congratulates itself on possessing in abundance. It is the echo of a lost voice, a message from the past that welcomes an empty future. 'The challenge of tomorrow . . . to reach out and fulfil our *squawk*.' Dreams.

December 19, 1982

Postcard from Munich

M Y LUFTHANSA Boeing 737, aided by what its pilot called
zer rather stronk vesterley vints, whistled coldly into
Munich airport on an afternoon so clear that the Alps were
picked out sharply in egg-shell blue under a premature pink
sunset transposed from a canvas by Altdorfer. In the winter
sunlight the lakes around the city shone like silver paint.
Ludwig II of Bavaria drowned himself in one of them, im-
pelled by a potent cocktail of schizophrenia and undiluted
Wagner. It was a bit premature to do likewise but I couldn't
help feeling depressed.

Narrowly personal though it might sound to say so, the
Nazis have always got on my nerves. It's almost the least
disturbing effect they ever had on anyone, but it was enough
to make me go on postponing my first visit to Germany. Mug
up on the subject but don't go there until the whole bad scene
is a back number: that was roughly the idea. So now, in early
1983, when to put off the trip any longer would entail a
decline into absurdity, not to say senility, I had arrived just
in time for the fiftieth anniversary of the Nazis' rise to power.
In Munich there was nothing except Hitler on or in all
media. Every bookstall looked like a photo call in Berchtesgaden. Turn on the television and there he was. This might
not be his town any longer, but he was still all over it.

History, however, should not be read backwards. Munich,
although founded as the Bavarian capital by the doomily
entitled Ludwig the Strict, was proverbially a jocular metropolis before Hitler rose to prominence and it has some claim
to have become that again since. Determined to see the city
in the most favourable light, I had chosen my time carefully.
In spring, summer and autumn the locals are famous for
wearing identical hats and short trousers, drinking even
more beer than usual, slapping one another's hands,

marching through the flower-filled streets and shouting '*Ahoi!*' So I had been careful to arrive in the depths of winter, when none of that would be going on.

For a first sample, there is more than enough jocularity in just the architecture. The Allied air raids reduced it to a sea of rubble, but much of it has been rebuilt with the special care lavished on the past by those who have been injured in the present. Where modern buildings had to fill the gaps, they were obliged to do so sympathetically. The result is coherent and appealing: a *mélange* of late Gothic, northern Renaissance, baroque and rococo, with much of the original disarming chaos neatly preserved in the grids of nineteenth-century neo-classical grandiosity imposed by the Wittelsbach dynasty in its later stages. The culture-conscious Wittelsbachs never ceased to make grand improvements, but the population was regarded almost as a member of the family and its welfare was not ignored.

The result was, and is, charm in depth. There are informal gardens, formal gardens, prospects of large public buildings, clusters of smaller ones, churches with knobs on, eye-tricking façades and acres of colour-washed stucco trimmed with white plaster. The whole gleamingly clean shemozzle is linked together at basement level by an antiseptic *U-Bahn* as good as Moscow's and a vast, interconnecting system of cellars in which people slap one another's hands, wear identical hats and drink beer.

Where other cities have a water table beneath them, Munich has a beer table. But in winter the noise is merely deafening and you can always walk on the surface, snacking on the world's greatest hot-dogs while enjoying the general effect of old Petersburg tangled up with Salzburg, plus the bridges of Paris.

Old Petersburg is a long way away but Salzburg is just over the mountains, from which the clear Isar comes flowing as fast as a man can run. The Bavarians aren't being presumptuous, just ponderous, when they call themselves North Italians. Even in cold weather there is a lightness to the view.

The English Gardens, laid out by an American adventurer who was ennobled as Count Rumford, have no greenery in winter, but the lakeside walks probably benefit from the absence of students, who in summer make obnoxious public love. Standard unisex kit for park-walking in the cold is a fur coat, space boots and a poodle in a tracksuit. The citizens of Munich are even more dog-crazy than the English, but have somehow trained their pets not to poo, thus materially aiding the impression that the whole city is cleaned and polished once an hour, like Disneyland.

The same applies to the Residenz, the official town house of the Wittelsbach family since practically for ever. Atomised by the air raids, it was put back together with tweezers just the way it was, which was pretty confusing in the first place. To symbolise the Wittelsbach family's enlightened regard for Culture with a capital K, the National Theatre cum opera house looms at the very entrance of the palace, reminding you that the world premières of several different Wagner operas helped to scramble Ludwig II's brains at short range. Wagner shouldn't be held responsible for Hitler's anti-Semitism, but he can't have been good for Ludwig's grip on reality. Even without the romantic music on the soundtrack, however, the residents of the Residenz would surely have tended to get carried away.

Once inside, the only thing to do is wander around lost for about a week. Succeeding generations of Wittelsbach Dukes, Electors, Princes and Kings remodelled the place for centuries on end, rarely throwing away what had already been done, so that you keep opening doors on another epoch. The Schatzkammer, or treasure room, houses the collection of baubles for which Albrecht V, who should have been called the Accumulator, laid the foundations in the sixteenth century. Trinkets aren't my favourite thing, but it's hard to argue with so many crowns. The hit item is a dinky statuette of St George slaying a dragon studded with emeralds, but there are another thousand almost equally lavish pieces to back it up.

The collection, the private property of the Wittelsbachs, was traditionally dipped into at times of heavy out-of-pocket expense. The family usually managed to stay within budget, but there was the occasional necessity to pay for the Thirty Years' War, subsidise Wagner, etc. Now that the family no longer rules, it can keep a smaller household and dress more quietly. Ludwig II, as well as his demented castles in the environs, built a winter garden on the roof of the Residenz and in full regalia looked like Oliver Hardy wearing a Gobelins tapestry topped off with a dead polar bear.

Of the many suites of rooms in the Residenz, the best were designed by François Cuvilliés the Elder, a court dwarf of the early rococo who happened to contain within his tiny form the heart of a great architect. All on his own, Cuvilliés would be sufficient reason for coming to Munich. Pieced back together after the bombing, the frail silver curlicues and pastel damask panels come springing to life around you as if the power of your eyesight were enough to start them sparkling. The strange feeling that you've seen it all before is not quite accurate, since even the Tsarist summer palaces outside Leningrad aren't as exuberant as this. You haven't seen it all before, you've heard it all later – in the music of Mozart, two of whose operas were premièred in Munich, one of them in the Cuvilliés theatre attached to the Residenz.

It is still attached to the Residenz, although to a different wing, the original auditorium having been pulverised by the bombing. But the panelling, which had been safely stored, is now reassembled inside a new shell. The previous central chandelier has been replaced by a group of smaller ones and the old extravaganza of a ceiling is now a flat panel, but otherwise the brilliant little theatre is as it was, a dimpled champagne bubble in which the spectator sits rapt while the surface glitters with tracery and cherubs blowing silent raspberries. It's all done with wood, plaster, paint and gold leaf, but it makes you feel wealthy, as if human fantasy had reached its highest stage, where the worthless becomes the priceless.

Mozart loved Munich and wanted a steady job, but he had struck the Wittelsbachs during one of their rare economy drives. Maximilian III, variously called the Good and the Wellbeloved, although never the Imaginative, liked *La Finta Giardiniera*, but said there were no vacancies. Max's successor, Carl Theodor, who perhaps should have been called the Unusually Obtuse, reacted the same way to *Idomeneo*. At a mere hundredth of what it later cost to keep Wagner in caviare, Munich could have been the Mozart city and left Vienna nowhere. History was all chances once, like now.

Chance dictated that the Cuvilliés theatre should be bombed to smithereens while two impeccably glum Nazi buildings on the Königsplatz were left untouched. Nowadays they are the School of Music and an admin block for the arts. The local guidebooks don't draw attention to their erstwhile functions, but by triangulation from other sources it was possible to figure out that those two long horrors in yellow limestone must be the Führerbau and Parteizentrale respectively. Built by Paul Ludwig Troost, Hitler's pet architect before the advent of Speer, they were once decorated with eagles bearing wreathed swastikas for eggs. The eagles are gone, but the balconies are still well placed for the ghosts of the Party hierarchs to watch phantom parades.

Having worked out which of the Führerbau's windows must belong to Hitler's corner office, I tried to look like a music student, walked confidently up the monumental interior staircase, and pushed open the door of room 105, in which the Munich treaty was signed. There was nobody in there except a Canadian girl called Monica practising the piano. Once the room had contained Mussolini along with Goering: a tight fit. Born in 1959 ('that's the year when all the stars were right'), Monica was ready to suspend her studies while I fossicked in the distant past. I stood on the balcony and reviewed a big parade of strutting spooks all wearing the same sort of hat. The door to the left must lead to Hitler's office. I eased it open and found a string quartet playing Schubert.

It was good to know that the corner office is nowadays filled with a more dulcet noise than the Führer giving dictation, but one's mood was all wrong for lunch in the Hofbräuhaus. Hitler's preferred hangout, the Bürgerbräu-keller, was discreetly obliterated in 1979, thus completing the demolition job which George Elser had begun with his sadly unsuccessful attempt on Hitler's life forty years before. But the Hofbräuhaus played host to the top Nazis often enough to give your Blutwurst an extra tang. The safest sausage in Munich is the albino Weisswurst: I should have ordered that, but after midday you are supposed to steer clear of it, since if, when cut, it doesn't sound like silk being torn, then it isn't fresh. But a Weisswurst ten years old couldn't be worse than a Blutwurst, which looks like a cross-section through a dead dachshund.

I don't drink alcohol nowadays, but sank half a mug of beer for purposes of research. Sinking all of it would have made me as drunk as the guys at the next table, who were all wearing the same sort of hat, slapping hands and shouting 'Ahoi!' Later in the year, during the Strong Beer Festival, a special brew called Kulminator is served, which apparently has to be drunk lying down. But if this was the Weak Beer Festival it was going well enough.

With spirits half lifted I journeyed to Nymphenburg, which lifted them all the way. Nymphenburg, the summer palace of the Wittelsbachs, lies within the limits of the modern city, which makes it the world's loveliest suburb. Starting off as a baroque edifice, it was a rococo paradise by the time it was finished. The landscape flows through the main building like a lake, lakes glitter in the landscape like mirrored floors, and there are pavilions full of mirrors like frozen waterfalls. Even in the winter, with the garden statues boxed against the cracking air and all the trees transparent, the place breathes prettiness.

On holiday from their heavy robes, here the Wittelsbachs could indulge themselves in the belief that only appearances counted. The extremely heterosexual Ludwig I was merely the last of several Wittelsbachs to adorn Nymphenburg with a Gallery of Beauties, but he gave the project his whole heart. All the best-looking ladies of the day had their pictures hung on the wall for royal contemplation. Carolina Countess von Holnstein aus Bayern, we may now note, had a waist the size of a wedding ring and shoulders like a Green Bay Packers linebacker, but her breakfast television pout still rings bells. Ludwig included a shoemaker's daughter and a ravishing Jewess among the noble pin-ups, thus indicating his belief in the democracy of beauty – a propensity which he overdid by falling for the hottest star in the cluster, Lola Montez. Less interested in the democracy of beauty than he was, she tried to dig a title out of him, whereupon the outraged populace forced him to abdicate.

But in Nymphenburg any monarch could lose touch with reality. If Ludwig the Strict had lived to see it he would have become Ludwig the Languid. Of the pavilions in the park, the most bewitching is once again by Cuvilliés, who built it for the Electress Amalia – hence its name, the Amalienburg. No bigger than the average cricket pavilion, it purports to be a hunting lodge, but is in fact just another example of Cuvilliés turning a confined space into an expanding universe of silver filigree and sparkling glass, a bubble chamber which one enters like an intrusive cosmic particle and departs from in all directions, the overdosed ego lost in the multiplication of its own image. A hot-shot for Narcissus.

I left Nymphenburg walking on air, which was bad training for where I was going next. The Amalienburg epitomises 1,000 years of Munich's history. The concentration camp at Dachau does the same for the Thousand Year Reich, which luckily didn't last the advertised distance, although it contrived to express itself memorably during the short time available. Dachau is a whole district, so the answer to the question why they didn't change the name is that it would be like changing the name of Clapham. But Clapham never had a concentration camp in it.

When the German word for concentration camp is shortened to its initials KZ, it appropriately comes out like a slap in the face: *kah*tsett. The snow was falling as I stood in my warm coat for a few minutes where the victims had to stand for hours and were beaten if they fell. There is not much left of the KZ except what might be called the reception building, which now contains an exhibition consisting mainly of the relevant Nazi official documents. These are not translated from the German, so the touring schoolchildren from Britain are likely to miss the full impact, which is perhaps fortunate. There is a letter from a mother in Ravensbrück to her son in Dachau. Prisoners weren't allowed to mention they were being ill-treated, on penalty of being treated even worse, so she couldn't ask him outright how he was. 'You must always remember', she wrote, 'that your life and health are indispensable for our future *and so important.*'

Und so wichtig. But that was in 1944, when the victims at least faced the relatively benign prospect of quick extermination. Before the war, the inmates of KZ Dachau were routinely tortured to death over a period of years. This was the university of the SS. All the big names who later administered the empire of misery got their basic training at KZ Dachau. They started off by murdering real enemies and moved on to murdering imaginary ones. Grown men screamed in long agony so that their tormentors could later congratulate themselves on dispensing a quick death to women and children. In the *Aeneid* there is a place called the broken-hearted fields. Standing in that snow-covered space I could think of no better phrase. Nor was there any point in self-reproach for being unable to shed tears. If we could really imagine what it was like we would die of grief.

Changing Dachau's name would have been pointless even had it been possible. The name of the whole country needed changing – which, when you think about it, was pretty well what happened. The Federal Republic of Germany is trepidatious at the thought of what a world recession might bring, apart from the two million unemployed it has brought already. Everybody is busy telling everybody else about Hitler, as if in fear that his significance had failed to register. But there are ample signs that it has sunk in.

Hitler's sole lasting positive achievement was to cure the old Right of its opposition to democracy. On its own, the Left has since been unable to convince anyone except itself that there is any better system. On top of a crippling reparations bill and a world-wide economic disaster, it was the ruthless pressure from either hand that throttled the Weimar Republic. As more of the story is painfully recounted, it becomes less and less easy to point the finger. But the important lesson has already been learned: once power has been seized, it is too late to protest, even for the heroic – and most people are not that.

Most people are not imaginative either, and can't be blamed for it. How much atonement is enough? The bombing must be allowed as at least part-payment: those of our young people who are concerned about the moral problem posed by the Allied air offensive should at least consider the moral problem that would have been posed if the German civilian population had not suffered at all. If the people of Munich were to live with the full knowledge of what was brought about in their city – if they couldn't walk past the Four Seasons hotel without imagining Hitler and Streicher meeting there in the early Twenties to share wild dreams of mass murder, or if they couldn't cross the Ludwigstrasse in front of the Feldherrnhalle without remembering that the SS ceremonial guard used to beat up anyone who didn't give a Hitler salute as he walked past – then the day's work would simply never be done.

As things are, Munich has a lot to be proud of. What could be rebuilt has been rebuilt. The great synagogue was not put back – Hitler tore it down deliberately long before the RAF could flatten it in passing – but that was mainly because there was nobody left to worship in it. There is a monument instead, saying: 'Remember this, your enemy mocked you.' What haunts Munich, as it haunts all Germany, is the presence of an absence. There is continual talk of *Kultur*. Every film director is a new genius. If Karajan and the Berlin Philharmonic fight over a new clarinettist it is headline news in the pop papers. But the Jews took the possibility of a first-rate contemporary culture with them. Hitler, preaching health and strength, made Germany blow its brains out to lose weight.

Yet Munich's past is rich enough to suggest, perhaps misleadingly, that the human spirit can survive anything, even a lobotomy. In the very ugly Haus der Kunst – another Troost masterpiece which unfortunately survived the bombing unscathed – Paul Klee's paintings now hang in honour where they were once hung to be mocked. If the Kandinskys in Paris put you off him, the ones in Munich will put you on: his life-long mistress kept his best pictures safe through the dark years and then gave them to the city. In the Alte Pinakothek the Altdorfer 'Battle of Alexander' is a pink and blue glory showing no ill effects from having spent fifteen years in Napoleon's steamy bathroom at St Cloud.

But there is a Rembrandt a few rooms away that tells you all there is to know. One of a sequence illustrating the life of Christ, it shows the cross being lifted up. The man in charge of the execution gazes straight out of the picture with all the arrogance of institutionalised cruelty. He has one hand on his hip and looks rather like Hitler. It is Rembrandt himself, facing the evil in his own soul. The main difference between him and Hitler was that he could see within. And paint better, of course.

February 13, 1983

Postcard from Jerusalem

A s the BA Tristar Stargazer Rose passed over the island of Rhodes and started the let-down into Tel Aviv, the late afternoon sky and sea shaded into each other with no horizon. So much haze suggested a lot of heat down there. The flat sea broke into a surf of white buildings. Ben-Gurion airport was half-full of commercial jets. It was also half-full of military transports: C-130s like the Entebbe raiders and rows of Dakotas harking back to the old gun-running days before the state of Israel officially existed. Planes from different wars, they looked the same age in the hot air.

Beside the road up to Jerusalem after sunset, the spines and carapaces of buses and armoured cars, painted with red lead and left there as memorials, looked ageless in the headlights of four lanes of traffic. In 1948 there was a single carriageway or even less and some of the bus convoys never got through. In 1938 the trip takes less than an hour by shared Mercedes taxi and the biggest risk you run is of being driven mad by the news programmes on the car radio. If the language is not Arabic then it is Hebrew plus static. The two tongues sound roughly the same if you don't understand them.

The American Colony hotel is in the eastern, *ergo* Arab, part of the city. My ambitions being those of a tourist rather than a foreign correspondent, I had figured out that in the event of a sudden war with Syria, Jewish terrorists would be less likely to blow up an Arab hotel than Arab terrorists to blow up a Jewish one. I was determined not to let history ruin my holiday. Besides, the American Colony is easy on the eye, with a fountain splashing in the flower-filled stone courtyard and cool rooms with domed ceilings ensuring sound sleep until a few hours past midnight, whereupon the mosque next door wakes up the faithful for prayer, and the unfaithful along with them.

The mosque has a minaret but no visible muezzin. Instead it has a loudspeaker system that sounds like a concrete mixer rigged to play very old Leonard Cohen records. Actually the broadcast material is a cassette of selected passages from the Koran, but unless you are a Muslim already the noise won't make you feel any more kindly towards Islam, so when day finally dawned I headed downhill towards the Old City determined to do Christianity, my old outfit, first. Islam could come next and Judaism last, it being, so to speak, the home team.

Just around the corner from the American Colony, the whole area of the Mandelbaum Gate is still pocked with bullet holes, reminding you of how much metal the two components of the populace are capable of flinging at each other during times of stress. People on the streets either were Israeli soldiers or weren't, in about equal proportion. The average soldier seemed barely post-pubescent but was made less laughable by a slung machine pistol or an M-16. Looking as much like a tourist as possible – the trick is to read map and guidebook simultaneously, while checking all street signs and regularly holding up a wet finger to establish the direction of the wind – I arrived at the Damascus Gate and plunged into the souk, the legendary Arab market where it is possible to obtain spices, nuts, dates, dark glasses and Dallas T-shirts.

Acquiring a sun hat for a price which left the man who sold it to me laughing in disbelief that I had agreed without haggling, I found my way to the Church of the Holy Sepulchre, built on the actual site, according to a revelation vouchsafed the saintly Empress Helena, of Our Redeemer's crucifixion and entombment. Golgotha is a rock sticking up through a split-level chapel to the right of the doorway. The tomb is under the rotunda and inside the Aedicule, a marble launch vehicle with a small, low doorway at which it is necessary to queue while waiting for the maximum four people within to get over their sense of wonderment.

The four people ahead of me were Japanese, with the

appropriate photographic equipment. They were inside for a long time and seemed to have generated an electrical storm, or possibly a small nuclear chain reaction. Then they came out stern first. This might have meant that they were Buddhists, but after going in there myself I concluded that they had merely been Christians with bad backs. It is a tight fit in the Holy Sepulchre and the arrayed silverware is not much compensation. The experience registered zero on my holiness meter but perhaps I was beyond redemption.

From the Holy Sepulchre I went out of the Old City through the Lions' Gate and across the Valley of Kidron to the Garden of Gethsemane, where the kiosk selling soft drinks at least has the merit of not claiming to be on the actual site of Christ's arrest, merely near it. After downing several tins of the Israeli version of Coca Cola – it calls itself just Cola but even that's putting it a bit high – I went up into the Mount of Olives, and thus reached the conclusion that if Jesus ever did the same he must have had strong legs. It is a near-vertical climb with few stopping places that aren't already occupied by goats, but when you look back across the valley you get some idea of why Royal David's City should have received so much media coverage in history both an-cient and modern. In a landscape shaped by the Creator with a blowtorch out of hot rock, the position of the city is the one unmistakable offering to Man. The onlooker's whole in-stinct, as his brain curdles under the noon sun, is to get inside and worship in any form that involves having a drink.

That night I got into training for my first encounter with Islam by watching a belly-dancer circumnavigate the swim-ming pool to the adder-lulling rhythms of a Palestinian pick-up band with amplified guitars. When she pinched the thumb and forefinger of her extended right hand together it started a ripple which set off a spasm in her left hip after crossing her chest like a mule-train through mountains. She was dynamite. She was also, I discovered after tucking a 500-shekel note into her bejewelled waistband, a Jewish girl who works every major hotel in the Middle East for a three-month season and then goes back to Los Angeles to run a workout studio. Pondering the mystery of existence, I was played to bed by the Koran cassette and fell asleep just in time to be woken up by it again in the darkness before dawn.

Back in the souk next day, I turned left past a merchant selling carpets printed with the image of Elvis Presley, had my bag checked by teenage Israeli soldiers at the entrance to Temple Mount, and stood suitably dazzled by the Dome of the Rock itself, the Qubbat al Sakhra. 'Where are we?' asked an American pointing a Panasonic minicam at the golden cupola. 'We're at the Rock of the Dome,' said his wife. Their attached name-tags proclaimed them to be members of the Samuel Group from Minneapolis. A guide told them about the Temple Mount. 'This platform was built artificially by Herod the Great.' 'By Harold the who?' asked the man with the minicam, pointing it at the guide. 'Herod. King Herod,' said his wife, taking a photograph of her husband with an Instamatic.

Feeling that my spiritual communion with Islam was being distorted by Western influence, I took off my shoes and entered the Dome, which isn't bad as domes go. The strict, Byzantine geometry of squares within circles comes as a relief after the eclectic shambles of the Holy Sepulchre, and lines from the Koran look far more beautiful incorporated into the scarlet and gold mosaic of the inner cupola's roof than they sound on a clapped-out tape-recorder in the middle of the night.

One of the two main reasons why the place was originally built was to impress the infidel and in the case of this infidel it worked. The other main reason was to provide a sufficiently grand shelter for the eponymous Rock, which, fenced off in the centre of the building, still protrudes at the same angle as it did when the Prophet departed from it on his Night Journey to Paradise. As opposed to the founder of Christianity, who ascended vertically like a Harrier, the founder of Islam needed a take-off ramp. There must have been a lot of air traffic over Jerusalem in the old days but presumably the departure times were staggered to avoid the risk of collision.

After sleeping at the hotel through the middle of the day, I was galvanised by the mosque clearing its throat and headed back into the souk, to be greeted from dark doorways by that strange, ullulating cry which means 'Here he comes again! The man who will pay anything!' Stopping only to consult my maps and guidebooks, I zig-zagged towards that corner of the city which held the Jewish Quarter until the Arabs captured it in 1948, whereupon the centres of devotion were flattened.

When the ruined area was retaken during the Six Day War, the Western Wall was taken along with it. To this, the holiest place of Judaism, I now found my way, hoping that it would at least provide, in contrast to the stereo minarets, a modicum of reverent silence. This proved not to be the case. What it provided was reverent uproar.

Against the gigantic and precisely fitted stones of the old temple platform, the Jews have been praying since 1967 in the attempt to make up for the years they were denied access. The men get the lion's share of the wall. The women must look on, but a gentile male needs only to have his bag checked and he may wander at will among the varieties of Jewish religious experience. Ancient Hasidim on little chairs sit so tightly against the wall that the brims of their black hats curl upwards at the front against the stones. The characters with the phylacteries on their foreheads are presumably even more orthodox, although if you didn't know that the little black box contained a slip of parchment you might think it was a battery pack. As the visitor ambulates past the praying backs from the open stretch of wall to the further stretch under Wilson's Arch, he must step carefully in order not to be bowled over by the bar mitzvah processions that pass at the trot every few minutes to and from the subterranean synagogue.

Most of the little boys being turned into men wear a yarmulka no more elaborate than a floppy frisbee and are thus outclassed for exotic flair by those young Hasidic devotees whose ancestry lies so far to the East that their unblemished oval faces, framed by unshorn locks, glow like Modigliani odalisques. Have they got sisters? As if reading my profane thoughts, an old man in full kit – hat, coat, book, beard – turns and looks at me accusingly every few seconds. But when I move aside he still turns rhythmically to look at the same spot. It is part of the routine. Whether he is expressing a personal quirk, or faithfully reproducing a special convention of prayer which was all his persecuted forbears had to call their own in some famine-racked Pale of Settlement *shtetl*, the onlooker would be unwise to guess. What the onlooker can't miss is the fervour. The Wall unites the various degrees and forms of Jewish orthodoxy into a single, throbbing hosanna.

Whether they can ever again be united away from the Prayer Place is another, and perhaps more serious, question. In secular Israel, State and synagogue are supposed to be separate, with the former providing enough dissension to be going on with. Internal religious quarrels were never on the programme, but hindsight reveals that they were inherent in a creed which places so much emphasis on the observance of the rules. The returning diaspora brought several different versions of the rules home. In the Russian Colony at noon on the Sabbath, I saw a man in a white kaftan and a climatically inadvisable fur sombrero shouting at passing cars. Apparently the only remarkable aspect of this behaviour was that he was not throwing rocks at them – standard practice in certain districts, which knowledgeable drivers avoid on Saturdays, and for most of Friday evening just to make certain.

The most integrated of these districts – almost, dare one say it, a ghetto – is Meir Sharim, meaning a hundred gates. In a few streets on the old border with Jordan, ten thousand Hasidim live in dedicated aloofness. The children look enchanting in white lace caps and the serene women in chaste peasant garb have a humbling charm, yet the men in full ultra-orthodox clobber plainly mean heavy spiritual business seven days a week.

Trinkets are on sale to tourists but there is no mistaking the fact that prayer is the principal manufacture. Visitors are told in advance not to disturb the mood. REQUEST AND WARNING TO WOMEN VISITING OUR VICINITY: NOT TO APPEAR IN OUR VICINITY IN SHORT GARMENTS (not covering the knee) IN SHORT SLEEVED CLOTHES (not covering the arm). THE TORAH OBLIGES TO DRESS IN MODEST ATTIRE THAT COVERS THE ENTIRE BODY. WE DO NOT TOLERATE PEOPLE PASSING THROUGH OUR STREETS IMMODESTLY DRESSED OR MIXED GROUPS PASSING BY TOGETHER IN MALE AND FEMALE COMPANY.

Such signs are hung above the street like parade banners. Watching a tiny man with unshorn locks, a long beard and at least three layers of black clothing inch past doubled up under the weight of an old Westinghouse refrigerator, I couldn't help feeling that the fear of defilement was being overdone. But a certain measure of hortatory self-assertion is understandable after a millennium of insecurity.

In sharp contrast to the way things were where the community originated, the Meir Sharim people cause the Government trouble rather than vice versa. Also they do it mainly by keeping themselves to themselves. In other parts of the city, even more orthodox groups browbeat the neighbours. During my stay, the merely orthodox residents of one district were complaining that if the ultras took over the filling station on the corner, no wheeled vehicle would be allowed to move unless drawn by a mule. Nothing so menacing from the Meir Sharimites. Any woman visitor dressed as a Carmelite nun in a gas-mask should be safe from attack as long as she doesn't accidentally stand near a man. The district exudes the unworldly reassurance of the cloister, if only because it is one of the few places on Earth where you will have difficulty encountering a child in a J.R. Ewing T-shirt.

But Eretz Israel was conceived in the kibbutz, not in the synagogue, and the diaspora didn't come home to be more holy, it came home to stay alive. Most of the founding Zionists, the ones who built up the country so that it could receive the mass influx when it arrived, were socialists from the Ukraine and White Russia who thought religion was on its way out of history. Some of the present-day Hasidim, on the other hand, are as anti-Zionist as Yasser Arafat, believing that deliverance can come only from the Messiah, and that Hebrew should not be spoken, only read. Such divergences could never have been pulled together even by the powerful beauty of the Torah. They were fused together, in the crucible of the Holocaust.

The secret of what made Israel into the last nation state is at Yad Vashem, on a hill outside the city. Like many building projects in Israel, Yad Vashem is bunker architecture, but in this case there was never better cause for showing the world a blank face. The Memorial Hall with its Eternal Flame is not as imaginative as Tel Aviv's splendid Museum of the Diaspora with its column of light, but it is still one of the world's only appropriate exercises in brutalist ribbed concrete. The roof weighs down on its thin rim of sunlight, the names of the extermination camps are spaced across the unyielding floor like a constellation of dark stars, and birds sing in the eaves as if one and a half million children had grown up to hear them, instead of vanishing into the smoke.

Whether all the young soldiers who have been brought here on the eve of battle were touched to the quick I don't know, but I can well believe it. My own imagination was unstirred, having been stirred to its limit by this disaster long before, or so I thought. But in the art gallery next door I was unmanned all over again, by one of the last works of Jacob Lifschitz in the Kovno ghetto, a drawing of a little girl. He drew her as if she were the meaning of life about to be subtracted from the world. Lifschitz perished in Dachau in 1944. Like nearly all the six million, he considered himself a citizen of the country in which he was born, with Palestine far away and the state of Israel not even a dream.

Hitler made the dream come true. He set out to kill a race and ended by creating a State. Everyone got the point except the Arab nations, who by belittling the magnitude of a historical tragedy, and continually threatening death to a people which believes such words when it hears them spoken, ensured both the expansion of Israel and a steady worsening of the Palestinian population's already desperate fix.

The visitor needn't leave Jerusalem to see what the refugees lost. Deir Yassin is within the precincts of the modern city. It is not meant to be a monument – there is no signboard to tell you what its name is or what happened there – but the valley of empty houses would make anyone wonder where the people went. The answer is that the lucky ones fled, and the unlucky ones were butchered by the Irgun. The leader of the Irgun at the time is the Prime Minister of Israel today.

Floating in the Dead Sea near where the Scrolls were found – they are full of thrilling messages about the need to send back the empty asses after the olive oil has been delivered – I was glad that the Middle East question was not mine to answer, since I was busy trying not to yell with pain from the amount of salt in my eyes, which I had been told to keep shut when I dived in, but had opened at the shock of bobbing to the surface like a suddenly inflated life-raft.

The salt gets into every orifice, but once used to the feeling of having been sodomised by a conical container of Cerebos I lay there as if on a hot, wet mattress and tried to take some comfort from the fact that with regard to the Middle East there is no advice which anyone of even vaguely British extraction can decently give, so there is no point getting into a sweat. If the British are not hated in Israel, it is for one reason only – that they made Israel possible, and out of altruism, not self-interest. The Balfour Declaration was the work of men who saw the need to redress a historic wrong, and their generosity is made no less admirable by the fact that it helped to create another one, which it will be for the Israelis to set right, as one day they must.

On that score Mr Begin needed no advice from a tourist. I spent most of my last night in the American Colony standing under the shower looking like Lot's wife but the chances were that the Prime Minister was awake too. The best and the brightest of Israeli youth had been camped every night outside his house demanding an explanation of the Lebanon adventure. Some of his colleagues were camped out there also, protesting against the protestors. The argument was keeping the neighbours awake like a mosque with a looped tape.

The minaret's pre-dawn gargle faded behind me as I went back in a shared taxi down the road to Tel Aviv past the fossilised convoys and the old Sherman tank on its plinth. At the airport security counter they made the Hasidic rabbi ahead of me open his suitcase. It held three more outfits the same as the one he had on. Then the Tristar took me back to the nice safe life that permits the luxury of laughing at the world.

August 14, 1983

The Queen in California

THE ROYAL Scuba Tour of California began last Saturday with scarcely any rain at all. The clouds over San Diego were full of water, but none of it was actually falling out of the sky as the *Britannia* edged towards Broadway Pier on the Embarcadero, just along from Anthony's Fish Grotto.

The surrounding area was heavily populated with members of the Secret Service wearing hearing aids and talking into their sleeves. Less numerous but more cheerful were the citizens of San Diego, some of whom were allowed on to the pier itself, at the end of which an honour guard of sailors and marines drilled with clattering M-14s, while E-9 Master

Chief Dye conducted the orchestra and frogmen were under water checking for bombs.

As things were to turn out, the frogmen were the only people appropriately dressed for the upcoming week of official events, but as yet nobody knew that. The American media were in position and fully equipped with Canon 600-45 telefoto lenses the size of garbage-disposal units and microwave dishes aimed at their very own relay helicopters, which were up there in the grey sky like benign vultures.

The British media were scantily accoutred by comparison but looked less scruffy than usual. Several of our photographers, though they had not gone so far as to put on a tie, had shaved only a few days before. Relations between the Palace and the British media had been strained by recent events, but with goodwill on both sides the special relationship could still be restored. As for the special relationship with the United States of America, the Queen and President Reagan would take care of that later, on horseback.

A 21-gun salute crashed out as the *Britannia* tied up. You couldn't help thinking that all the explosions might be setting a bad example, but out on the water the voices of dissent were limited to one small boat carrying the rubric GOD SAVE THE QUEEN FROM NUCLEAR ATTACK. This was easily countered on shore by such friendly messages as BODY BEAUTIFUL CAR WASH SAYS WELCOME QUEEN ELIZABETH. The lady thus addressed carefully negotiated the gangway. Her pearly queen frock was too thin for the weather but the pain-trained royal constitution made light of the discomfort. As for the Duke, he was in naval uniform with fully faded gold braid: very Falklands factor, very stiff upper teeth.

With the Reagans saving themselves up for later, the welcoming committee of lesser dignitaries could be rapidly dealt with. The Royal Couple then climbed into a COM-NAVSURPAC Admiral's barge to inspect the harbour, across which small squalls were skittering as a portent of bigger things. Somewhere out there in the rain sat the aircraft-carrier Ranger, with a single Tomcat parked on deck to indicate American air power. Lunch for the royal party would be served below decks, but first there would be a reception on the *Britannia* for the media, including the British media, who had all rushed back to the Holiday Inn to pick up their engraved invitations, clean their fingernails and tweeze out those ugly superfluous facial hairs.

This event was a big plus for the British Press. The ground rules were that nothing the Royals said should be quoted, but one of the American radio reporters nastily went on the air straight afterwards and said that the Queen had made a dull remark about the wet weather. Since only the presence of a canvas awning over the deck had saved everybody from being washed into the sea, Her Majesty's remark was scarcely inappropriate, but that was a minor consideration beside the fact that the American media had made the British look comparatively well behaved.

Brimming with self-righteous fervour, the British Press from then on were Royalists to a man. Although it was too early to say that the Palace and Fleet Street were as one, nevertheless there was a palpable sense that the Brits were all in it together, if only in their native capacity to sneer at, nay revel in, the rain. The Californians, by sharp contrast, were in a panic, having counted on the standard sunshine for a number of alfresco events, culminating in the famous horse ride during which the President, an A-picture leading man at long last, would finally and incontrovertibly get the girl.

On Sunday the Royal Couple lunched in a foursome with Mr and Mrs Walter Annenberg in Palm Springs. In his erstwhile role as US Ambassador to the Court of St James, Mr Annenberg evidently endeared himself to the Monarch through his unique command of the English language, by which his house, when he had the builders in, became a domicile undergoing elements of refurbishment. The Queen must have dug Walter's act in a big way, since it now cost her a flight and two motorcades in each direction just to get more of it.

Back at the *Britannia*, which had meanwhile moved north to Long Beach, she changed clothes for the biggest event of the week not counting the horse ride, namely the jumbo dinner in Sound Stage 9 at Twentieth Century-Fox. There was more rain on the way, but her spirits must have undergone elements of refurbishment in Palm Springs, because instead of ordering the Captain of the *Britannia* to set course for England she voluntarily entered the limousine that would take her to break bread with Marie Osmond, the current Tarzan, the man who used to be Davy Crockett, and at least two of the Gabor sisters.

These and several hundred other guests arrived by limo, stepping out under an awning while the shivering media, under nothing but the wet night sky, took notes and fired flashbulbs. 'I've had the priviledge' said Henry Kissinger, 'of meeding the Gween before, bud id's always a special oggasion.' The limos being a block long each, it took a while for all the guests to be delivered, even though Chuck Pick, chief executive of Chuck's Parking, took personal charge of the platoon of carhops unloading the precious cargo. Chuck made up in histrionics for what many of the guests were too old to manage. Fred Astaire was one of the younger luminaries present. Some of them had risen from the grave for the occasion but they had more in common than mere immortality. Gradually it dawned that they were nearly all Republicans. The Democrats were at home, seething. When Nancy Reagan finally welcomed the Royal couple, she was shaking hands with practically the only invitees who hadn't voted for her husband.

Inside went the Royals with the First Lady attached, leaving the media out in the rain with about a thousand security personnel and the terminally hysterical Chuck. The British media took shelter for the several hours that would elapse before they were allowed in to catch a brief glimpse of the uncrashable bash.

Your reporter found himself huddled under a wooden staircase with a tabloid gossip famous for never having written a sentence both true and literate at the same time, and a photographer who carries an infra-red lens for taking pictures of the Princess of Wales through brick walls at night. I was starting to see things from their point of view. When your subject matter is inside eating, it is not nice to be outside suffering. But when we eventually got inside it became clear that the guests had not been having much fun either.

The Royals were seated with the British filmstar colony all along one side of a long table up on stage, like a Last Supper painted by Sir Joshua Reynolds. Before and below them stretched a sea of Americans all staring in their direction. It was a stiffening circumstance in which only Dudley Moore could possibly look cheerful, although Michael Caine was also trying hard. Jane Seymour looked very attractive, which was more than you could say for Anthony Newley. Rod Stewart, clad in a black and gold John Player Special pants suit, sported an extravaganza hairstyle that left his wife Alana's coiffure looking like a crew-cut, but facially he resembled an ant-eater who had run out of ants.

The Duke was talking to Julie Andrews. In between the Queen and the First Lady sat Tony Richardson, looking very calm. Later on it emerged that this was because, having not been apprised of the *placement* until he was about to sit down, he had died of fright.

To have expired was to be fortunate, because the Entertainment now began. Emcee of the Entertainment was Ed McMahon, Johnny Carson's straight man. It is conjecturable that Carson would be lost without McMahon, but there can be no doubt that McMahon is lost without Carson, who was not present, having stayed at home because of a wisdom tooth, or perhaps because of wisdom. McMahon introduced Dionne Warwick as a Great Song Stylist. For the benefit of the Queen and other strangers, he explained what a Great Song Stylist was. A Great Song Stylist was someone who was not only a singer with Style, but a stylish singer with Greatness.

Ed took so long over the introduction that Dionne felt compelled to deliver an extended set. She was breathtaking if your breath is taken by a display of technique. She clapped her hands and swayed her hips. Gene Kelly, seated just in front of me, did neither of these things. Nor did the Queen, but she evidently quite liked George Burns, the next act on. George also went on too long, but at least he was himself. Frank Sinatra and Perry Como pretended to be Frank Sinatra and Dean Martin, doing that endless medley which is a good joke if the previous numbers have been kept short.

The Entertainment had elephantiasis, like the evening in general. When Hollywood gets beyond energy without taste, it arrives at taste without proportion. Perry ruffled his hair to prove that it really grew on top of his head, even if it had started its life somewhere else. 'You obviously do *not* adore me,' Frank sang at the Queen, who if she didn't nod her head, didn't shake it either. The big night out was a downer, but it wasn't her fault. They had put her on display.

In fact she had been had. The evening was a pay-off for Ronald Reagan's financial backers, who would never have met the stars if the stars had not come to meet the Queen. Buckingham Palace had been hustled into bankrolling the next campaign wagon.

But if the Queen felt manipulated she didn't show it. The rain was sufficient proof that not even the President could fix everything. It fell all night and on through the next day. Sections of California began dissolving into the sea. Lady Susan Hussey, the Queen's Lady-in-Waiting, packed away the silk frocks and laid out the macintosh, the boots and the sou'wester. If necessary, flippers and breathing apparatus could be flown out from home. It was time for a show of True Brit – the truly British grit not soluble in water. Up in the Sierra Madre at the British Home for old people, the lawn squished like spinach quiche. The media stood in it ankle deep while Her Majesty met an old lady in a wheelchair and received a quilt for Prince William.

The awed *Time* reporters, all wired up like the Secret Service, talked into one another's hearing aids through their sleeves, but the Queen had already moved on to the City of Hope Paediatric Hospital, there to be met by the founders, these latter including the inescapable Zsa Zsa Gabor in a royal purple fur coat, taken from some species of animal to which she probably represents the sole source of danger. The hospital had been specially repristinated at a cost of $100,000, much of it spent on the water-based paint which had been carefully applied to the gutters, down which it was now flowing.

On the way north to Santa Barbara next day, busloads of media shone pearly headlights through the solid white rain. The sea was full of mud and far too rough for the *Britannia* to leave Long Beach. The Queen's visit to the Rancho el Reagan was still on, but she would have to fly to Santa Barbara instead of sail and there would be no horse ride. It was a cruel disappointment for the British media but having caught the spirit of True Brit from their Monarch they were stoic in adversity. Even Paul Callan of the *Mirror*, a gossip columnist with the literary sensibility of a vampire bat, had been heard to squeal 'She is *our* Queen!' at some importunate Americans who had tried to get between him and his Sovereign. The *Mail*'s Peter McKay, compared with whom Callan writes like Congreve, had a moist glint in his tiny eyes which could only be tears of pride, since it was not yet raining inside the bus.

Behind us, the coast road crumbled into the waves and a tornado punched a large hole in downtown L.A. Up ahead at the airport, the President waited inside the Tracor Aviation hangar for the Air Force DC-9 bearing the Royal Party to come sluicing in under its own power. There were several hundred spectators, all chosen by the White House for their Republican views. I was on top of a filing cabinet with a trainee cheer-leader called Tuesday Pflug. A nice girl who had already met the President ('I have Ronald Reagan germs on my hand!') she had never even *seen* a Democrat, except in police bulletins.

The plane pulled ear-splittingly into the hangar, the Reagans glad-handed the Royals, and they all motorcaded off towards the hills past the happily sodden crowds and such signs of greeting as WELCOME TO GOLETA QUEEN ELIZABETH GARAGE SALE 26,000 ITEMS NEW AND USED. The American media kept describing the onlookers as subdood but who isn't subdood when submerged?

The media contingent for the ranch climbed into the assigned ground-clearance vehicles and after a thought-provoking trip up roads like rapids they debussed to discover a specially installed set of outdoor telephones wrapped in polythene. They also discovered that although there was no horse ride, the President had dressed as a cowboy anyway. He looked radiant, like a man who receives a visit from the Queen of Great Britain and Northern Ireland on the very day that the Dow Jones Index goes up 19 points. Starting to tell the Press all about it, he was cut short by the Queen, who after jeeping 2,400 feet up a mud mountain to eat a plate of re-fried beans might perhaps have begun wondering about the point of it all. Dimly visible through the mist, the backsides of two riderless horses glistened in the adjacent field.

But the Queen and the President had ridden together in England, and if Reagan gets re-elected they will no doubt ride together again. Back went Her Majesty to spend the night in the *Britannia*, still stuck at Long Beach. Thence next morning she commuted to San Francisco in Air Force Two, the President's spare Boeing 707, which landed in a plume of jetwash as the drenched media cowered on a flatbed truck. When the Queen stepped down to meet female Mayor Feinstein, the rain magically ceased. 'She's smiling!' cried a local television front person. 'That's a first!'

The merry mood intensified when the Queen checked into 46 rooms of the St Francis Hotel, because the media were staying there too, although only in one room each. The American media started interviewing the British media about whether this sort of thing happened very often. The British media, who were getting to like being interviewed, casually suggested that it happened every day. Suddenly all the limelight switched to their star, James Whitaker, who had arrived from London and moved into the studios of San Francisco's very own KRON-TV. Billed as Royal Reporter James Whitaker, he immediately established a special relationship with KRON's beautiful anchor-person Jan Rasmusson. 'Edward VIII,' he told Jan, 'was a person who put his own feelings ahead of duty.' The Queen, he made it clear, wasn't like that.

Whitaker's magisterial tone sealed the alliance between the Palace and the British media. Nothing could now keep the San Francisco stopover from being a success, even if the water level at the Alviso sewage treatment plant went over 9 ft and automatically dumped the raw effluent of a million people into the bay.

When the Royals plus Nancy snuck out for a quiet dinner at Trader Vic's, they found Whitaker already there talking to the cameras. Next morning there was a show at Symphony Hall that left the Twentieth Century-Fox Entertainment for dead. Tony Bennett sang 'I Left My Heart in San Francisco', a song that makes little sense if the singer is in San Francisco at the time, but what the heck.

That night in Golden Gate Park there was a protest rally involving 136 separate organisations, one of which consisted of a bearded man in a lace ball gown, but as the Royals and the Reagans sat down to a State dinner for 250 guests, including Joe DiMaggio, it was clear that the Scuba Tour had turned into a hit. The memories, as they say locally, Will N. Doer.

March 6, 1983

Around the World in
One Pair of Shoes

LAST SATURDAY morning when British Airways Concorde Flight 193 for New York taxied out to take off from Heathrow the coveted fourth seat on the flight deck was occupied by myself. My first Concorde flight was starting well. BA, having noted that I would be flying the flag on the opening and closing stages of my planned three-day flight around the world, was unashamedly after a good review.

It was in the bag. For my so-long longed-for, first-ever flight through the sound barrier I would be sitting up there among the lights, dials and digital read-outs. Usually the most glamorous young lady passenger gets the privilege and there were also several self-made British businessmen who had impressed me by their deportment in the Concorde lounge. 'No *way* I'm pain a secrecry nine arf fousand,' one of them had said loudly into the courtesy phone. 'For vat much *I'd* be a secrecry.' Once on board, another tycoon had handed the air hostess a suit-bag saying, 'Can I have this back before we land? On account of I have to make a quick exit.'

Twice the speed of sound wasn't fast enough for *him*. Undoubtedly the activities of either of these thrusting entrepreneurs were more essential to the national welfare than my strange mission, about which Captain Massie, as we waited for clearance to take off, frankly confessed himself puzzled. 'Why the whole world in one go?' I gave him the only answer I had ready. 'I just wanted to make sure it was round.'

The young co-pilot's response was something I had always wanted to say. Suave in dark glasses, he said it very well. 'Three, two, one, *now*.' An easy line to overdo. The runway rolled towards us while from a long way behind came an amplified version of the noise an electric train makes crossing Sydney Harbour Bridge. 'Rotate!' The co-pilot was getting all the best lines, but the air-traffic controller's voice through the headphones had a good supporting role. 'Set course direct for the acceleration point.'

With three computers in charge and her 130,000 horse-power on a tight rein, the beautiful aeroplane dawdled upward at only a few hundred knots towards the point, 28,000 feet above the Bristol Channel, where she would be allowed to let rip. 'From up where we cruise you can see the curve after sunset,' said the captain, politely still considering my problem. 'Believe me, it's round.'

Time to pump the lamp. The engineer pushed the four throttles forward with one hand. The pointer on the ana-logue Mach meter moved but almost nothing else did. That was it. Supersonic. After about Mach 1.1 you couldn't even feel her tremble as she went faster and higher all the time towards Mach 2 and 58,000 feet. 'It's a very potent motor,' said the co-pilot, who ought really to have been in movies but was probably too butch. The avuncular Captain Massie smiled tolerantly. It was clear that the Concorde's pilots have a good time. BA pilots who do not get to fly the gracile glamour-puss call her variously the Bionic Toothpick, the Poisoned Dart and the BAC Fuel-Converter, but would probably admit envy if pressed.

Back in my seat, I considered how long it took Magellan, almost half a millennium before, to get started on his pro-posed circumnavigation of the globe. Financed by Charles V, who wanted only 90 per cent of the take, Magellan left Seville with five vessels, having been helped to chart a course by Ruy de Faliero, the astronomer. But Faliero was also an astrologer, and after casting his own horoscope he decided not to go. He foresaw death. It might have been death from boredom, because after five weeks Magellan had still not even got his fleet clear of the river mouth and out to sea. But what Faliero saw was death from danger, of which there was certain to be plenty.

The chief danger I now faced was from too much comfort. The Concorde is sometimes called cramped but in fact it is just snug. You aren't in it long and anyway it lengthens by 10 inches when the racing airstream heats it up. Meanwhile the steak is excellent and the champagne copious. Very aware of the unemployed, I quelled pangs of conscience with the thought that my taxes had been paying the thirsty beast's fuel bills for the previous decade, and that in most respects I was travelling light. Where Magellan had five ships, I had one tote-bag with three shirts, three pairs of underpants, three pairs of socks and a copy of *The Magic Mountain*, this last to be read during any long waits in airport lounges. My portfolio of first class tickets was just to ensure some sleep, otherwise I would be unable to write up my log at the other end. Magellan never had that problem. He got a sound sleep from exhaustion every night.

Invited back to the flight deck for the landing, I strapped in just as Concorde began a long diving right turn back from the stratosphere and Mach 2 towards a low altitude, 300-knot extended holding pattern that had the pilots muttering imprecations at the Kennedy tower. 'Request longer vectors.' 'Negative, Concorde.' At her least fuel-efficient in such a nose-up attitude, snootily she guzzled gas. 'She doesn't like going slowly,' said the co-pilot, still getting all the best dialogue. 'It's no problem, but it's wasteful.' There were rain clouds but we were signalled down before they broke. The runway swung up and pulled us in. Kennedy was crawling with wide-bodies. We were a needle among haystacks.

Killing two hours and a Silex of coffee in BA's Monarch Lounge, I read half a page of *The Magic Mountain* before picking up the *New York Post* to read about the Miss America disaster. Vanessa Williams, the reigning Miss America, had posed nude for *Penthouse* and forgotten to tell anyone. Now she must resign before the offending pix were published. Pondering the evanescence of fame, I transferred through the rain to the United Airlines terminal for my flight to Hawaii *via* Los Angeles. A short woman with a big behind was shouting at her son, who was called Scart, as in Sir Walter Scart or Scart of the Antarctic. 'Scart! Come here, honey! Come *here!*'

She also shouted at her husband, who was standing right next to her. Praying for a seat near someone else, I trudged on to the aircraft, which I was mildly nervous to discover was a DC-10. Nobody had been killed on a DC-10 for some time but there are an awful lot of seats even up at the front and if you get pinned against a window it can be awkward. Luckily the aisle seat next to me stayed blank. There was a video tape to demonstrate safety. It fouled up. 'Welcome to the friendly sk . . . section . . . front of . . . *blup*.' It started again. 'Welcome to the friendly skies of United.'

For dinner I wisely chose the duck, but I shouldn't have eaten the sourdough roll. The movie started just as we passed over Kansas City. It was *The Bounty*, an excellent film about Captain Bligh's ambition to circumnavigate the globe. For 31 days he had tried to round Cape Horn in vain. In vain I tried to suppress the repetition of the sourdough. The movie ended somewhere over California. As we descended over the freeway into LAX, my shoes felt tight. United had not issued the usual enticing little cloth bootees, so I had not taken my shoes off, because getting them back on again can be a problem after the feet swell in the dehydrated air. Another hazard that Magellan never faced.

Nursing an orange juice in the cocktail lounge while waiting for the flight to resume, I read another sentence of *The Magic Mountain* before picking up the *National Enquirer*, which had so many stories about the errant Miss America that I was still reading it when I got back on the DC-10. This time the aisle seat beside me was full, and how. At 2 p.m. local time, or 10 at night on my internal clock, I was facing my first big challenge to the successful completion of my voyage. He must have weighed three hundred pounds and looked twice that in his black silk Hawaiian shirt writhing with electric-blue flowers. It was Menehune Fats! With a Mai Tai clutched like a thimble in one giant paw he conked straight out. Getting past him to the toilet would take grappling irons.

The movie made things worse. It was *Terms of Endearment*. Before leaving, I had agreed with the Editor that only a movie starring Elliot Gould, or two movies starring Burt Reynolds, would be considered sufficient reason to abandon the expedition, but Shirley MacLaine and Jack Nicholson blending egos was a severe test. Also I had eaten too much papaya, the only fruit on Earth, in my experience, which actually *tastes* yellow. But Magellan, after naming the Pacific, had taken 98 days to cross it with nothing to eat except rotten biscuits. When those ran out, the crew ate oxhides, sawdust and rats. United had treated me a lot better than that and I was duly grateful to arrive in Honolulu safe if swollen.

Until now I had been travelling through an extended day but at last it was night. It was too long before my next plane to hang around the terminal and not long enough to do the town, so I booked a room at a hotel within the airport perimeter. It was 15 dollars cheaper than the Holiday Inn but it had air conditioning and a bath. An alarm call woke me at 1 a.m. and I switched on the TV to make sure I stayed alert while repacking my tote-bag. *A Bridge Too Far* was on the Late Show, but just as Sean Connery was landing by glider there was a flickering transition to a porno picture featuring a naked lady practising fellatio on 20 male appendages protruding through a paper screen. From the visual evidence she was not having much success. A chorus of ecstatic groans from her disembodied clients suggested otherwise. I left them all to it and caught a Singapore Airlines 747 bound for Hong Kong.

The seats in the nose of a 747 are arranged in pairs but are so big that you enjoy the pampered solitude of an enthroned boy emperor. Singapore Airlines reinforces this impression by providing twice as many air hostesses as any other airline. For religious reasons they serve you one-handed: hence it takes two of them to do anything. I had always assumed that this was the reason why there are so many of them but apparently it is not so: the real secret is low wages. If they are broke, however, it doesn't stop them being beautiful in their damascene uniforms of hip-hugging sarong plus fitted, waisted jacket. Since cabin service sells the airline, the girls are a big plus. The hot towels they provide are up to JAL standards – i.e., not only hot but wet, so that after steaming your face you can flap them to make them cold.

Bootees being provided, I took off my shoes. This would be the longest stage of the trip – 10 hours plus – and the feet would inevitably swell. The rest of my body would swell to match unless I staved off every second meal. The seat reclined to the horizontal. Seven hours of oblivion supervened. When I opened the sliding window shutter it was dawn on the sea of cloud; pink-tinged on the streaked surface, puffs of lavender-blue cream underneath, and the depths shaking from turquoise into lapis lazuli. 'Did you have a good sreep?' breathed a lovely face. Oh yes.

Opening *The Magic Mountain* I found Hans Castorp drained of energy, so that each day in the clinic consisted of nothing but meals and the space between. His knees didn't work. Mine still did, but only just. When we landed at Hong Kong I got my left shoe back on all right but the right one popped its stitches at the side.

Hong Kong was my big stop – from dawn to dusk. BA had arranged a press conference in a suite at the Hilton, so that the local media could ask me what I thought I was up to. This promised to be a major embarrassment but there would be several hours before the inquisition started, so I limped down into the Wan Chai district in search of someone who could mend shoes. An ancient man who had been doing nothing else for a century was sitting on a box. He wore sandals, an apron and little more. This was a sensible approach to the torrential humidity. I sat on another box, took off my shoe and handed it over. He took a look and got to work, bodging a fluted spike through the little holes and then threading strong twine through the spike. A dab of polish and the job was done. Five HK dollars. In Britain it would have taken a week and cost more than the shoes.

Once again evenly shod, with my shirt a wet rag, I walked through the fish market, where most of the fish are alive until you point out the one you want. Hong Kong is Computer City but you can still watch a woman gut the fish you will eat for dinner. That was what I told the bright young television man with the American accent and the quiff: that the world had grown smaller without necessarily becoming bland. Just because it was now one world didn't make it all the same place. The young man smiled nicely and told his crew to wrap up. No doubt he was wondering how the philosophical stuff would go over on a channel devoted mainly to the sort of Kung Fu movies in which the hero wears black flared trousers and the soundtrack makes a noise like a tree being cut down every time he hits someone.

A nice girl called Anita packed up the glasses and the drinks the media had not drunk. For those who want to leave Hong Kong it now costs 400,000 American dollars for the so-called 'investment visa' that will get them safely away. The half-million people who make Hong Kong tick already have their getaway papers. The other five million are stuck. Anita is one of them. For a bad moment I felt like one of those rally drivers who go swerving dustily through an African village. The bad moment recurred at the airport because there were three big pictures of Mark Thatcher up on the wall. Billed as MARK THATCHER: RACING DRIVER, he was modelling Giordano tee-shirts and looked dauntless. In the city his father calls Honkers the same spirit perhaps no longer prevails undiluted.

How nice to have a home to go to. From here on it was a BA 747 all the way. Once again I was asked to the flight deck, for my very first takeoff in the cockpit of my favourite heavy. Taking off from Kai Tak can be either interesting or very interesting, according to the wind. If you take off up through the hills it is very interesting because you can look into people's living rooms. If you take off out to sea it is merely interesting. We took off out to sea through the suddenly dark night but made an immediate 180° climbing turn so as to head back across mainland China. With the turn complete I could see a pool of glowing cloud cupped in the hills of Hong Kong Island and Kowloon. It was shot through with the light coming up from the city, a junket of electric mist.

I had been to Hong Kong before, on the way out of China. It had been like coming back to life. The life was not so much in the glittering shopping malls of the Central district as in the hustling tumult of Wan Chai, where you can see a mechanic squatting on a box as he repairs a Ferrari Dino in a workshop so small that the tail of the car sticks out into the street. There are two-room electronics firms with washing hanging out of the windows. There are men who will repair your shoes. It is all very productive and all very untidy, and one day those mystical pedants from the mainland, who know what history should be like, might get the urge to neaten the place up.

Yes, I had been here before, going the other way. So with a long way left to go I already knew for a moral certainty that the world was round. When Magellan died in the Philippines he had the same certainty for a comfort. He had been there before, and therefore knew the way home. Not that it would have been quite as easy for him as it was for us. The captain dialled the course into the inertial navigation system and the aircraft headed for Abu Dhabi. I went downstairs to my reclining seat for a meal and a movie. The movie was *Footloose* and I watched it half asleep, which was apparently the way it had been made. Then a few words of *The Magic Mountain* put me out completely.

When I woke up and looked through the window I could see fires at the bottom of the dark: oil platforms in the Gulf. Still in my bootees I lurched up the spiral staircase to the flight deck and strapped in just in time for the approach to Abu Dhabi. The lights of the 13,000-foot runway lay on the blacked-out desert like a bejewelled Jugendstil hair-clip.

When we touched down I thought there had been a mistake: the 747's cockpit is so high up that you feel there must be another 50 feet to go. 'This is still the only really great people-mover,' said the co-pilot, true to the BA tradition by which the first officer gets better dialogue than the captain as compensation for less seniority.

Topologically speaking, the terminal at Abu Dhabi is a torus – a doughnut of which you inhabit the inside surface. This is completely rendered in mosaic tiles, like a Byzantine particle accelerator transformed into a bathroom. It was here that the retiring captain, who had been even more avuncular than the captain of Concorde, introduced me to his successor, who was more avuncular still, like James Robertson Justice without the beard.

I had a fresh crew for my last leg to London, but in my case they did not have a fresh passenger. Strapping in on the flight deck for the take-off up into the seemingly perpetual dark, I was a hard man to impress or even contact. Nevertheless I was wowed all over again as we rolled like a tall building on castors down the extravagantly long bowling alley of lights. Captain, first officer and engineer all grew six arms each and the sum total of their button-punching sent us up to where, under the dome of the stars, a rim of soft white light ran around us far away, with nothing holding it up except darkness. I thought it might be dawn but the engineer said it was the ozone layer catching the starlight.

The engineer seemed very boyish although no more than the first officer. Nor did the captain, despite a great show of wry eyebrow and booming voice, look anything like what must be his true years. Flying keeps them young. Perhaps if I could work the controls it would do the same for me.

All I could control was my reclining seat. Expertly depressing the lever, I moved smoothly into level flight. The movie was *Splash*, an entertaining nonsense about a mermaid out of her element. On land she grew legs, but had to be back in the sea inside six days. After almost three days in the air I had not grown wings, but got ready to become earthbound again with some regret. To my own satisfaction I had solved the mystery, and in doing so risked disappointment.

On 27 April 1521, almost two years after Magellan's enterprise began, the only surviving ship came home. She was the *Vittoria*, commanded by Juan Sebastian del Cano. He must have been a world-weary man. I like to think that Ruy de Faliero was waiting on the dock. What a meeting: one of them worn out from having actually been there, the other still excited with the possibility. If Faliero had been less the astrologer and more the astronomer, he would have realised that his science was the true magic and gone in search of adventure.

But he would have found it hard to maintain his enthusiasm. Once the imagined thing is done, it takes more imagination to bring back the excitement. In just my lifetime, long-distance air travel has stopped being an event and started being a cliché. But a miracle is no less miraculous for having become commonplace. Faliero's celestial maps and Magellan's heroic generalship are still there. But they are deep inside the instruments and the computers. One of the things that writers do, I think, is to recapture the old strangeness that lies hidden in the new normality.

Perhaps the price of wanting to do this is a childish nature. After sleeping like a small boy worn out by too much Christmas, I woke somewhere above Frankfurt to be regaled with BA's catering triumph: a jumbo version of the old country's chief culinary treat, the British Railways breakfast. How the ingredients for this had been obtained in Abu Dhabi defied explanation. I ate two lots of everything except the fried tomato, and thereby put the finishing touches to what would be, by the eye's reckoning, a net gain in weight of about ten pounds for the trip. Of the 18 men who survived Magellan's voyage, few would have had the same complaint.

Back on the flight deck, the windows were alight with the slow dawn of Tuesday morning. We were scheduled for an autolanding but one of the transmitters on the ground got its wires crossed, so the captain took her down hands-on. As we banked over London I could see the *Observer* office where they had a hole in the page waiting for my copy. Then we straightened up, jacked out the flaps, and went in, parking right next to Concorde, which was getting ready for the run to New York. Using my index fingers for shoe-horns I finally got my shoes back on, but spent a lot of time bent double.

July 29, 1984